Daily Telegraph
VEGETABLE GARDENING
MADE EASY
VIOLET STEVENSON

D0263515

COLLINS
GLASGOW AND LONDON

William Collins Sons & Co. Ltd.
London & Glasgow

First published 1976
Reprinted 1976

© *Daily Telegraph*

ISBN 0 00 412067 1
Printed in Great Britain

CONTENTS

Introduction   5

1 It All Lies in the Soil   7

2 Tools and How to Use Them   17

3 Space Makers   30

4 A Warm Soil Gives Better, Earlier Vegetables   36

5 ABC of Vegetables   43

6 Calendar of Garden Work and Crops Available   102

7 Personal Touches   111

8 Pests and Diseases   119

Index   123

INTRODUCTION

Vegetable gardening is currently very popular, as evidenced by booming sales of vegetable seeds and the great demand for allotments. This intense interest is not simply the result of economic pressures and the consequent need to save money. The urge to grow food is partly the result of the realisation among many of us that we have a responsibility to those in other parts of the world who do not have enough to eat. Most of us have been and still are wasteful of food that could save lives and, looking at the complexities of distribution, we tend to shrug off vague feelings of guilt. But they remain, and I suggest that this subconscious acknowledgment of responsibility plays its part in sending us out into the garden or on to the allotment to grow food for our own families. Indeed, I feel we should consciously nurture this feeling as a means of motivating us.

There are other benefits, however, all free of charge and all of which might incur high costs. The exercise, gentle or strenuous according to capability or desire, might have had to be gained under expensive supervision at gymnasium, health farm or even clinic. The fresh air might have to be purchased for brief periods in the mountains of Scotland or on distant beaches. Grow your own vegetables and you will get both exercise and fresh air free!

But best of all, I believe, is the revelation that you can achieve unknown flavours and textures when you taste for the first time vegetables that have been grown in your own soil. There's extra nourishment, higher vitamin content and freedom from artificial additives – but these are celebral matters. Flavour is a basic physical pleasure which is dependent on several things but mainly on freshness, the freshness that can only come from growing your own.

I have been a gardener all my life and a vegetable gardener for most of it. In this time, I have made mistakes, faced disappointments, and suffered disasters. But I still cultivate my own vegetable garden and the reason is that it gives me enormous pleasure, pleasure in growing and pleasure in the crop. Most of the following pages are recollections of this pleasure and I only hope that some of it will rub off on to the readers.

1

IT ALL LIES IN THE SOIL

If you have never grown vegetables before do not become intimidated by the technical terms and the scientific or even traditional jargon employed. Do remember that through the centuries many people have produced their own food by doing little more than sowing seed or planting tubers in comparatively unprepared soil. Just as you can serve up a good meal without being a fully qualified chef, so without being a skilled horticulturist you should be able to produce enough vegetables in variety to give real pleasure and satisfaction at a cost which means real economy.

However, it seems a waste of time and effort to use hit and miss methods if better ways can be found, especially if these prove in the main to be easy, inexpensive and certainly more productive. Quite simply, the best way to grow succulent and abundant vegetables is to ensure that the soil is well cultivated and rich in plant foods. The quicker the plants grow the more tender and better flavoured they will be, an invariable rule which it will be helpful always to bear in mind.

The well-being of the soil is in your own hands. Its care and cultivation does not call for scientific knowledge nor long training on your part, but it does ask for understanding, for the realisation that soil is alive and that it constantly needs replenishing. Its cultivation need not entail great expense, as we shall see, but according to circumstances the preliminaries to making a kitchen garden may take time and effort. This depends upon the condition of the soil. Actually it may not be necessary for you to go to a great deal of trouble. In most cases, because the garden lies on ordinary soil and because this has already been cleaned and even cultivated, perhaps for lawn or flowers, it offers no particular problems in preparation. In such cases the gardener can simply go out, fork over the plot, lime or feed it and plant or sow right away.

Indeed, the lazy or the ignorant gardener can do just this even with the poorest and least cultivated of soils and probably gain some kind of a crop. But results are likely to be so meagre in comparison to what can be gained with very slightly more attention that they are proved to be uneconomic.

There are exceptions, however, and the following remarks on soils in general have been included at the beginning of this book so that they may help those who feel that they may have a problem on their hands or those who wish to obtain a high yield of tasty and nourishing produce. This does not pretend to be a scientific book, so I have tried to keep information and advice as simple and as brief as possible. Neither is it a book advocating or explaining the production of 18in beans or 2lb onions, but urging instead the growing and harvesting of small, tasty, nourishing and tender vegetables quick and easy to cook and sweet on the palate.

Kinds of soil
Generally speaking there are, physically, three kinds of soil: light, medium and heavy. We speak of heavy and light soils in much the same sense as we speak of a cake being heavy or light, which is to say that the heavy one lacks air spaces. These soils are composed of sand, clay, peat, chalk, and humus and, of course, most are mixtures, for if soil were purely of one material it would not be fertile. Well mixed soils are called loams. A loam should be a mixture of sand, clay and humus, although loams can vary according to district and may be sandy, chalky, etc. Rotted turves make a good loam.

If you know your wild plants you can often get a quick rough guide as to the type of soil on which they grow. Loamy soils will produce chickweed, possibly abundantly. I knew an old gardener once who showed no sympathy with anyone who complained that chickweed was a nuisance weed in the garden. 'It's a poor soil,' he would say, 'that can't produce a crop of chickweed in winter.' Groundsel, fat hen, the annoying goosefoot or cleavers and sowthistles will also be prevalent. (I have gained some satisfaction in writing these words, having just come in from my own garden where I had been forced to weed out these very plants. They would not have been growing on the same soil a few years ago.)

Beware if you see moss growing on the soil surface, for this flourishes on 'sour' soils and where drainage and aeration are at fault. If bracken is present the soil is acid.

Chalky, clay, or sandy soils, as their names suggest, are those in which the chalk, clay, or sand predominate. Fortunately most soils are 'ordinary' and the majority of plants do excellently on them. Ordinary or neutral soils are easily made a little more limy or acid when this is necessary. Where there is a definite type of soil as described above, the gardener should aim to introduce other ingredients to make a better balanced mixture. Fortunately this is not a difficult nor an arduous task. Ideally, soil should contain equal parts of sand and clay with plenty of humus and enough lime to correct any acidity. We can mix such soils specifically for use when we grow plants in pots. These potting soil mixtures are given the name of 'composts', a confusing term because it is also applied to the mixture which one makes from decaying vegetation to use as a mulch or manure. Very few, if any, garden soils are perfectly balanced and after all the crops we grow on them are bound continually to alter the balance. This is why we have to keep watch and supply certain ingredients ourselves if we want to extract the full value from our gardens.

Clay soils

Although most soils contain some proportion of clay, and often in a garden you will find one small area which has much more clay than elsewhere, the term 'clay soil' is applied to most heavy, sticky soils. Clay soils are usually cold and because of this the crops grown in them are later in coming to maturity than those grown in warmer soils. This is important when you hope to raise winter vegetables, salads in particular, and so for this reason alone it is worth spending some time and effort on improvement. Soils with a large percentage of clay are often badly drained. You can see that this is so because water remains on the surface for some time after rain and it is impossible to walk on the soil without it adhering to the soles of your shoes. Sometimes such soils are even waterlogged, which means that they become very sour because they are never aerated. It is these soils which need certain intensive preparation if they are to be made both productive and easy to work. One good thing, clay soils are usually rich in plant foods although they do entail initial difficulties. Apart from anything else, a fork or spade full of clay is much heavier than one of loam, which means that digging is hard work. It is my experience also that these heavy, difficult to work soils harbour difficult to eradicate weeds such as convolvulus and couch grass, now fortunately, thanks to weedkillers such as Weedol, easier to clear. Clay soils also harbour slugs, as do any heavy moist soils, sometimes even those which contain lime.

As I said earlier, you can improve the condition of such soils mainly by altering their texture. For instance, fibrous materials and animal manure which contains plenty of straw, when dug into the clay soil will help to open and aerate it. Lime has a wonderful physical effect on heavy soils, because by its means the clay flocculates, in other words becomes crumbly instead of remaining close and sticky. You can see this same effect on clay soils which have been left in lumps when dug in autumn. The action of frost and wind breaks down the clods and reduces the soil to fine crumbs, but without the lime this condition is not maintained, so you can see that a good deal of lime needs to be applied to heavy soils. Do remember, however, that lime should not be used at the same time as manure because one counteracts the other. An interval of at least six weeks should elapse.

Sandy soils

Sandy soils, on the other hand, are light and easy to dig. They are warm and produce early crops. As you would expect, they are easily drained, but this can be a drawback, for the rain water passes through the ground so rapidly that it leaches out, that is bears away, plant foods with it. Furthermore, sandy soils dry out too rapidly in hot weather. In this case, para-doxically perhaps, to make sandy soils heavier we should add to them much the same ingredients as we add to heavy soils to make them light. Animal manures are excellent, but in this case the heavier types of dung are best, i.e., cow and pig in preference to horse and stable manures.

One should remark in passing that animal manures should be stacked and allowed to rot for several months rather than used fresh from the farmyard. Usually by this time their character has changed. They have become more like soil or rotted garden compost in appearance and are more pleasant to use. As well as animal manures, other organic sub-stances such as lawn mowings, vegetable refuse, seaweed and peat can be used, but more about these later. All of them simply supply humus to the soil. This is an absolutely essential ingredient, without it no soil is fertile.

Acid and alkaline soils

Acid soils are the opposite of alkaline soils. They are those in which there is no lime or chalk or very little. Some soils are slightly acid and adjust-ment is relatively easy, but there are others such as peat land that are extremely acid. Few plants will grow in very acid conditions. So far as a vegetable garden is concerned one should take care because soils which have too much manure applied to them often become too acid. This is one reason why it is useful to test the soil from time to time. Acid soils need to be given plenty of chalk or lime in some form or another at the necessary intervals. Most garden crops thrive best in soils which are very slightly acid, or in those soils which are neither too limy nor too acid and so are described as neutral. Fortunately most soils are 'ordinary' or neutral and it is easy to adjust them to suit a particular crop. For instance one can dust the soil along a row with lime either before or after sowing seed, where this is desirable.

To determine acidity or alkalinity soils are tested for their pH value, a complex mathematical symbol which I find easier to accept than to explain. The neutral figure is pH 7.0. Below this figure the soil is more acid and as the figure descends they denote the increasing degree of acidity. As they ascend they indicate alkalinity. Ideally, garden soil should have a pH value of between 6.5 and 7.0. Danger zones are below 5.5 or above 8.0. The reason why such readings are alarming is that below pH 5.5 many crops just cannot grow, and above pH 8.0 we can expect to find many plant disorders. These are usually due to the fact that certain essential plant foods or minerals cannot be absorbed under such alkaline con-ditions.

It is possible to test soil yourself by means of simple soil testing kits of which there are several types on the market, or it is frequently possible to send samples of soil for analysis to your County Horticultural Adviser, to the Royal Horticultural Society or one of the major garden chemical manufacturers. It is quick and easy to test your own.

It really is important, where you suspect an unbalanced soil, to determine its condition. If the soil is acid, the acidity can be corrected by adding lime, but here again one should be cautious because an excessive use of lime can do as much damage as no lime at all. Where a garden exists on ordinary soil it is usually sufficient merely to dress the soil with lime when sowing or planting certain crops. Details are given for these as they are dealt with later in this book.

We talk of soils being 'sour' and as I remarked earlier such soils often are covered with moss, the presence of which is usually an indication that the soil needs draining. In such soils harmful kinds of living organisms flourish, even sometimes predominate. Often deep and efficient digging and liming will adjust matters, especially if this is followed by wise cultivation, which includes constantly adding suitable organic materials to the soil to provide humus and stimulate helpful bacterial activity.

Chalky soils

One might imagine that really limy soils by contrast would be good, but this is not so. Soils which have too much chalk in them will not grow good crops. Although there are certain chalk loving plants, only few of them are vegetables. Chicory is a chalk lover. If you are on chalky soil see that it is well drained, otherwise it may become very sticky in wet weather. Deep digging and the introduction of plenty of humus will help rectify this condition.

Sometimes the soil may lie in a shallow layer over a bed of chalk. In this case you should try to deepen and enrich this shallow layer. This entails digging into the chalk below and incorporating materials with plenty of humus into it. In addition to this, or if you cannot or do not wish to dig, you can build up the top soil layer by means of mulches constantly applied. And, of course, the more you mulch the deeper the top soil becomes and the richer in animal and bacterial life. Some of the humus and the associated benefits will inevitably be taken to the lower levels by some means or other and so gradually the soil will become deeper and deeper and better and better.

Improving neglected ground

My own vegetable patch is now on a piece of ground which had been neglected for so many years (if indeed it had ever been cultivated) that in summer it dried to the hardness of concrete. When I tried to thrust a spade into it this would rebound and sparks would fly! Now this same soil produces wonderful crops including the succulent asparagus. The improvement was brought about by the use of simple materials which were all around us. First of all, because we were busy with other things, my husband and I simply cut the few poor weeds which grew there and let them rot on the surface. Then we gradually added grass mowings and left these to rot also. At times when it became possible to dig the area, usually after rain, we neatened it and dug in the rotted mulch and gradually added leafmould and garden compost. Drills for the first vegetables were made and lined or filled with peat. When I planted brassicas each planting hole was made a little larger than necessary and filled with a little well mixed and rich soil prepared previously. We used plenty of lime. As the vegetables appeared above ground, all except the potatoes, which were gradually earthed up, were liberally mulched between the rows with lawn mowings. These were kept an inch or so away from the actual plants. The mulch kept the soil beneath moist, it helped to smother weeds and made good pathways when one gathered the crops. By walking on the grass mowings the soil did not become panned or solidified. When the crops were cleared the mulch was either drawn to one side so that a new seed drill could be made in the moist soil it had been covering, or it was forked into the soil.

If you are beginning absolutely from scratch you will not have a store of well rotted compost, nor many lawn mowings. Fortunately the popularity of pony riding has provided plenty of stable manure, some of it processed and conveniently packaged and there are a number of other products with an organic base which are excellent soil conditioners. These organic dressings are extremely easy to apply and most are quick acting. They help give body to light soils and to make heavy ones more friable.

Rich soil is essential and I am sure I could not crop my own garden the way I do if I did not feed it so generously, but one must remember that richness is according to degree. Some vegetables go on developing just as we hoped they would when they are grown in rich soil, but there are others, parsnips for example, which if they are grown on newly manured soil will produce masses of roots instead of the one desired neat, well-shaped tap root.

It is well worth bearing in mind that if you have reason to believe that your soil is poor you can adjust matters later by feeding your plants while they are growing. Naturally all will do best if they are given a good start.

Compost

I like to compare the garden with a bank account, and I draw the parallel by saying that you cannot continuously draw money from your bank without reducing the sum originally deposited there. It is the same with your soil. You cannot continuously crop from it without reducing its available resources. So you must try to put back into the soil as much as you take from it.

One of the best and most natural ways of doing this is to use your own home made compost. This is, as you probably know, simply decayed vegetable matter, leaves, kitchen waste such as peelings, the remains of flower arrangements, lawn mowings, hedge trimmings, soft weeds and the leafy tops of such perennial kinds as possess harmful roots, fallen leaves and even the contents of the vacuum cleaner bag. You should not compost diseased matter such as potato haulms from plants affected by blight, or rotting onions and the like. When it has finally rotted down the compost should look like well matured leafmould. It should be odourless and pleasant to handle.

Do not hesitate to spread small seeding weeds on the heap, for even if some of these should germinate their lives as young plants are very short. The heat generated in the heap soon kills the seedlings.

All the materials mentioned above are assembled in a neat pile and this can be simply as its name implies, a composite heap, regular and rect-angular if possible. However, there are certain drawbacks to such sim-plicity. If you lace your compost with organic waste, eggshells, fish bones and skin and kitchen waste generally, you are likely to find that it will be turned over by certain furred or feathered scavengers who will not leave it neat and tidy, but who will destroy the outline of the pile and strew its contents in the vicinity.

So the best compost heap is made from a box-like container which will hold the contents in one place yet allow air and some moisture in to help the rotting process. You can buy ready-made compost bins fashioned from several materials or you can easily make one yourself from timber, bricks or wire netting. You will find it convenient if one side is removeable. Dimensions will depend on the size of your garden and the quantity of refuse available, but in general it will usually be best not to reduce the heap to less than about three feet square to allow space for the materials to heat up and rot down effectively.

You make the compost heap this way. To begin with make a layer at least six inches deep at the base with heavy twiggy material. This will allow air to flow under the heap and at the same time it makes a drainage layer through which moisture generated by the heap or rain water can drain away. On this base place all the soft vegetable matter and after this has reached a depth of about nine inches cover this with about two inches of fairly fine soil. Continue making layers of this kind until the heap reaches the top of the bin, In practice you will probably find that the actual top is seldom reached because as the materials rot down they settle and the level sinks.

It is important that the compost should not become waterlogged, and for this reason you will find it helpful to cover it with a lid of some sort. On the other hand the compost heap should not be allowed to become too dry or bacterial activity and the rotting process will not take place properly, so in periods of drought it is wise to water it occasionally, using about a gallon of water to every square yard of surface.

Special compost accelerators can be bought which when spread, applied or watered in as the case may be will not only considerably hasten the rotting process but will also improve the quality and richness of the final compost. All of the leading garden chemists sell their own brand of accelerator. Or you can use your own preparation by treating each layer of about six inches with a little nitrogenous fertiliser such as sulphate of ammonia and some lime, each applied at a rate of about ½oz. per square yard of surface area.

You will usually find that the centre of the heap rots down quickly and leaves the outside still much in its original state. For this reason it is helpful to turn the outside to the centre, usually in about a month or two depending on the season. A way to facilitate this is to have two compost bins side by side and to transfer one to the other as the compost is mixed. Without a second bin I suggest that you will find it most helpful to spread a plastic sheet on the ground nearby. The compost can be forked out on to this and you will easily see which portions should go back into the centre to rot further.

Bonfires

Too many gardeners light too many bonfires, which besides often being a social nuisance greatly reduce the 'savings' which could and should be put back into the garden bank. It is important to realise that much more value can be gained by composting green materials than by burning them, so do not be tempted to clean up quickly this way. Actually a neat compost heap is many more times cleaner than a smouldering fire which pollutes the atmosphere and which leaves you little in return except a burned patch of soil which cannot for some time be used to grow anything.

It is true that the ash that is left yields carbonate of potash and also minute quantities of minerals, some of which, known as trace elements, are substances which are essential to plant life, but the ashes can vary considerably. Those left by one bonfire may be nothing like so rich in the amount of potash they contain as those from another. So much depends on what has been burned. Generally speaking old wood contains the most potash, as much as seven per cent., but the ashes from the average garden bonfire might contain as little as one per cent.

We save the ashes from the log fires we burn indoors in winter and use them on certain crops. The only bonfires we make are of materials which cannot or should not be composted, such as twigs and hedge trimmings of the woody type, large prunings, diseased plants and pernicious weed roots. The ashes are always saved and spread on the garden as soon as possible. It is important, incidentally, that these be used as soon as they are cool and before they have been weathered. If they cannot be used right away, cover and store them, because if they are exposed to rain the precious percentage of potash will be washed uselessly away.

Coal ashes should not be dug into the soil except if they be very gritty as from a furnace, in which case they can be incorporated into very heavy soil to make it more open. Some people use coal ashes along pea and bean drills to discourage mice, but generally speaking they are best used for spreading on standing grounds or for making paths if they have to be used at all. Unlike bonfire ash, always allow coal ash to weather if it is to be used on the garden, for it contains injurious minerals which need to be softened by rain.

Fertilisers

The subject of plant fertilisers is a little more complex than is generally supposed. There are two attitudes of mind, one school which supposes that it is sufficient to buy a packet, can or bottle of fertiliser and apply this to the soil at the recommended rate, and the other which believes that farmyard manure or home made compost is the best fertiliser and no inorganic or manufactured products are necessary. Both are wrong.

In the first place it cannot be said strongly enough that manures and composts, however well rotted and prepared, contain only minute amounts of plant foods. Their importance, their vital importance, is that they condition the soil so that bacterial and fungal activity is accelerated, a condition in which plants can most easily accept and absorb the plant foods present in solution in the soil. Bulky manures and composts, rich in humus-making materials, are vital to the well-being of soils and soil structures and hence vital to the well-being of plants.

Inorganic fertilisers, manufactured chemicals, will enormously boost the growth of plants if applied correctly but they do nothing for the soil itself and so after a time they cease to be effective. They must be used in conjunction with humus making manures and composts if they are to benefit the plants in their vicinity.

The most frequently used garden chemicals are sulphate of ammonia, sulphate of potash, muriate of potash, nitrate of soda and sulphate of magnesium, to mention only a few. The average gardener probably tends not to use these basic garden chemicals but a balanced mixture, probably sold under a trade name. These proprietary fertilisers cost a little more than the basic chemicals, but they are frequently produced with an organic (usually peat) base and they have the great convenience that being balanced they can be used to feed any type of garden plant. Yet although they are so easy and convenient to apply, they must never be used carelessly and certainly recommended doses should never be exceeded or damage might be caused to plant roots or foliage.

The basic chemical most necessary to plant growth is nitrogen, increasing the speed and strength of development to a significant degree. Organics available, mainly nitrogen based, include dried blood, quick acting, and hoof and horn, longer lasting. Inorganics include nitrate of soda, nitrochalk, sulphate of ammonia and urea-form, a highly concentrated form of urea and formaldehyde which is long lasting.

Phosphates are mainly useful to develop the root system of plants and are provided organically in bone flour and bone meal, and inorganically in superphosphate of lime and the slow acting material known as basic slag.

The best form of potassium or potash for plants, the fertiliser that promotes the growth of flowers and fruit (and according to type, vegetables) is sulphate of potash, quick acting but also long lasting. Wood ash, containing potassium carbonate, is also useful as mentioned above.

These three are the major or most important fertiliser ingredients and are generally known by their chemical symbols, N, P and K. Consequently, when buying a bag of balanced fertiliser one might see these symbols followed by figures indicating the percentage of each chemical contained. Sometimes, in fact, the NPK will be omitted and one might see simply the figures 16:5:5 for a high nitrogen fertiliser or perhaps 4:6:8 for a fruit fertiliser. An average well-balanced fertiliser for nearly all crops might have a safe content of, say, 7:7:7.

In addition to these basic plant foods certain others are required in lesser degrees and of these the most important are calcium or lime (necessary as a plant food as well as a soil conditioner) and magnesium, particularly helpful with some fruits such as tomatoes. Trace elements are required only in the smallest quantities and are normally provided in balanced fertilisers. They include boron, copper, iron, manganese, molybdenum, sulphur and zinc and they need be of little concern to us normally, as the provision of good humus making materials and balanced fertilisers will usually give a sufficiency of these trace elements.

2

TOOLS AND HOW TO USE THEM

I imagine that the first concern of most new gardeners is not so much the structure of the soil as how to get the plot in working order. Not all plots, unfortunately, are there waiting nicely levelled and free of weeds. Obviously you will need tools. There are a few traditional types which are essential. Basically, garden tools have altered little through the ages, possibly because methods of gardening have changed little either. You could get by with an absolute minimum of a digging fork and a dibber, which is a pointed stick used for making holes for planting. This also could be used for scratching or marking shallow seed drills or channels in the nicely dug soil and the fork for taking out larger drills, but I suggest that you will find work easier if you add a rake and a hoe. Work can be made easier still if you gradually add to these so that in time you have a good spade, a trowel, a variety of hoes and two kinds of digging fork, one light and one full-sized.

Do not rush out to buy a number of garden implements for which you have not yet found a need. You are likely to find that you use two or three much more frequently than the others.

It seems to me after a lifetime of gardening that the most important thing is to make your work as easy as possible, both because it is more pleasurable that way and because it will leave you energy to do more! Therefore the tools I use most frequently are light in weight. I prefer modern tools which have been designed with function rather than tradition in mind, and where full use has been made of modern materials and manufacturing techniques. You can see what I mean if you lift a really old-fashioned spade and then take a modern stainless steel example.

If you continue to use heavy tools you will expend much of your precious energy merely on wielding them. When you go to buy any, keep this point in mind and test all the tools for weight. Those with long handles such as rakes and hoes should ideally be some 6–9ins less than your own height for comfort and efficiency, but if you find that longer or shorter than this seems to fit your movements better or fatigues you less, go by your own comfort rather than general practice. Many tools are now also made of substances other than wood. You can have them with aluminium alloy handles and plastic covered finishes that are both pleasant to handle and easy to keep clean. They wear and weather well and they will not break even though they are nothing like so heavy as wood, especially when this gets damp.

Modern finishes are frequently brightly coloured, which means that they are noticeable when left in the vegetable garden or on the lawn after you have finished using them. They can then be collected, cleaned and taken to shed or garage for storage overnight. In spite of their modern finishes these tools are bound to deteriorate if left in the open in all weathers at all times. There is also the not unimportant fact that when tools are neatly stored away in their usual places they can be picked up instantly when you go to use them next, whereas if they are left in the garden where they were last used a few precious minutes will be wasted in searching for them.

Tools for digging
Let us begin with digging, and first, the tools which are used for this operation. You can use a fork or a spade, and if you can afford only one of these tools I suggest that you buy a fork. The usual type has four flat tines or teeth and they are made this way so that the soil will remain on the fork as it is lifted out of the ground and turned over. The advantage of a fork over a spade is not only that it is lighter in weight but that it is also much easier to push into the soil. It is also more useful for levelling the dug soil surface than a spade. On the other hand, some people like a spade better because they say that with this they can remove a neater, more solid mass of earth, and when they dig a spit deep (the depth of their spade) they can remove all the soil from the bottom of the trench, which is also cleanly cut. And of course if you garden on very light and friable soil you might find a spade more convenient simply because this soil would fall between the tines of a fork if you dug when it was dry.

Perhaps I am biased because I was taught to use only a fork for digging when I worked on a commercial nursery. Certainly I saw no one else there using a spade for digging large areas, and there was a fine row of shining bright forks always hanging up in the shed. The guvnor insisted that forking was quicker and aerated the soil better than if a spade was used.

Obviously the longer the tines the deeper you can dig, but I know that the very size and weight of a full-size digging fork deters a number of people from attempting to tackle this part of gardening.

I should perhaps point out here that there is a good range of specially designed tools intended to eliminate or lessen the pain and labour of digging. Many of these are the results of work carried out by the Disabled Living Foundation, with whom manufacturers and designers have co-operated. So if you want to dig but have difficulty or suffer discomfort in doing so, or even if you are partially disabled even to the point of having to sit for most or all of the time, do remember that there are tools designed to help you. You should be able to inspect them or see illustrated catalogues and so to buy or order them from any good garden centre.

A general purpose lightweight fork

For general use I have a lightweight fork, known as a border or lady's fork, and I would recommend its use to all those, men and women, who find gardening heavy though enjoyable work. Obviously, being slightly smaller than the normal size it does not lift such a heavy mass of soil and it cannot dig and so cultivate the soil so deeply, but you can reach a compromise on this, as I hope to show, by building up on the basic soil to make up for the lack of penetration below. The only occasion when I do not use it in the kitchen garden is when I need to lift long, deep-set roots such as parsnips and leeks, in which case I use the full man-size fork. Apart from the fact that this more easily lifts up the entire root intact, there is always the possibility that you might break the shaft of a small fork by forcing it to do the work meant for the more strongly made tool.

My little fork is so easy to handle that I use it for many purposes. In some cases it is more efficient and easier to use than a hoe, for example when I want to make a wide, deep drill for peas. Traditionally we are recommended to draw out such a drill with a hoe, but unless you have very light, friable soil, this can be hard on the tummy muscles, shoulders and back. With a good, strong garden line and the little digging fork it is a matter of only a few minutes to take out the soil and then to draw the tines along the bottom of the small trench to level it. As you would expect, on very light soil a small spade can be used in the same manner and I must confess to having and using a lady's spade as well as a fork.

The same fork is as easy to use as a rake and often more effective when one is clearing spent crops, potato haulms, or pea vines for example. In such cases the fork can be used to draw the debris along the ground and then to lift it into the barrow or on to a strong plastic sheet, as the case may be, to be carried away.

I use it also for many tasks connected with harvesting. I prefer to lift shallow rooting vegetables such as beetroot, shallot and others in dry weather, and at such times I can give the soil a little extra attention while I am in fact carrying out another and separate task. Any weeds which have been overlooked can be prised out at the same time. It is so much easier to use a small fork like this when you want to do such things as lift and clear cabbage and brussels sprouts plants which are too well anchored to pull out, but which, I think, do not warrant the use of the full-sized heavy fork.

There are other types of lightweight forks. There is the manure fork, often with five tines which are rounded so that they can easily be pushed into a pile of dung or garden rubbish, but as a rule a manure fork is not strong enough nor properly designed for digging, although I must say I have seen it used quite effectively on heavy land by someone who found it made the work easier and was kinder to the back. There is also a modern lightweight fork described by the manufacturers as a bedding fork and recommended for use on stony ground. Small stones often become fixed or wedged between flat tines and are difficult to remove.

Digging: for and against

Before we embark on digging perhaps we should ask ourselves, why do we dig? Some people claim that we are wasting our time doing so and it is interesting to note that there is at this moment a question along the same lines being asked by the farmers, are they right to plough?

The introduction and the wider use of the paraquat and diquat based weedkillers indicates that they might do better to kill the surface weeds, sow their seeds among the vegetable debris and leave the rest to nature. Certainly I have seen some fine crops grown this way. I have not experimented sufficiently myself on a plot of land which has received no digging at all to be able to relate my experiences, but I do know that the soil does remarkably well without half the attention that is said to be necessary. This suits me, because as the years go by, I find that I tend more and more to look for easy methods. On the other hand I see a lot of truth in the old adage that lazy people take the most pains. Fortunately, easy gardening is not lazy gardening.

I think that many of us dig the ground because this makes it look tidy and I wonder how much we shall appreciate a landscape of fields brown with untidy, fading plants when we have come so much to enjoy the furrowed texture of a well-ploughed countryside. But it may come. I suggest, in fact, that many of the heavy digging operations we are urged to undertake in our gardens are simply a hangover from another age, and are usually advocated by those who gained their training at the hands of gardeners who had in turn been taught traditional methods only and had never thought to question them. Once, labour was cheap, and being plentiful it sometimes happened that there were more gardeners than tasks for them to carry out. You can keep a gang of gardeners, even the very young ones, quite busy, hence out of mischief, and warm into the bargain on a frosty day by putting them to deeply trench and ridge a large empty plot of land. Whether you would demand this if you had just one man, or if you would find it necessary if you worked on your own is another matter, but in this way custom becomes established.

Instead of digging it is possible to get the necessary improvement of the soil structure and bring it to the essential tilth required for good seed sowing in the upper few inches, by adding organic materials in the form of mulches. The fact that this practice also lessens your labour by cutting down the necessity for weeding and for watering is a bonus. Scientists have shown that the important factor in the fertility of the soil lies in its structure. Their researches also indicate that the more the soil surface it disturbed the less fertile it tends to be. Instead of lightening and aerating the soil, digging and ploughing are now said to create a pan or hard floor just under the surface which inhibits the passage of air, moisture and even of roots.

However, in a book of this nature it is not my intention, nor my role, to set out to prove a theory, merely to share my experience and to offer some advice to those who seek it, but I do intend to describe any easy methods I know of and which I have found to be successful. Obviously I must explain how to prepare a garden in the traditional manner, for there will always be those who would prefer to have it so, but I would like to add that I truly believe that those who have an established garden and who are beginning to find much of the work over-demanding, should consider slipping into the stream of easy gardening and to concentrate by conservation, to add to the soil rather than spend time and energy on breaking it up. This is what I am doing in my own case. Had I known earlier what I know now (a lament we have all uttered at times) I think that I should have gone about making my garden in a different way. I certainly would not have become involved in such hard labour. There are so many short cuts once you accept that there are other ways than digging to reach your goal.

For example, take the cultivation of potatoes. It has been accepted for some years that an efficient way to clean ground, especially where you are planning a new garden, is first to grow potatoes on as much of it as is possible. The various operations involved keep disturbing the ground so that it becomes well dug and weeded. First, the ground is dug in whatever manner the gardener thinks necessary, which can include ploughing or rotovating and not necessarily digging by hand. Pernicious weed roots are removed, the soil levelled and the tubers planted. As soon as growth shows above ground the land is earthed up so that it gradually becomes ridged, which means that a large surface of it is exposed to the weather. As the earthing up is done, emerging weeds are killed. Finally, the potatoes are dug, the haulms removed along with any more weeds that have appeared, the soil is levelled and the result is that the plot is well dug, nicely cleaned.

A more modern and labour saving method is first to spray existing weeds on the plot with Weedol in solution with water. This weedkiller acts only on the green tissue of the plants and does not affect the soil in any way. The plants gradually turn black or brown, they die and rot and their debris is pulled under the soil by worms. There is no harm to soil, insect life, bacterial action and no residual effect. Using a garden line and a hand trowel the tubers are planted in lines and spaced in the usual way. When the shoots emerge above the soil they are earthed up, and if before this more weed seedlings should appear, these can be treated with Weedol. Only when the potato plants are actually growing should we cease to use the weedkiller or we should use it with great care so that none touches the green growth of the potato plants. By using a narrow sprinkler bar applicator we can weed between the rows or along the ridges should this be necessary. We continue earthing up the plants as required, for unless we use black polythene sheeting (see Potatoes) this operation is demanded by the fact that some tubers grow on the soil surface and turn green under the influence of sunlight and are thus made inedible. Finally we dig the crop. The ground is still cleaned and cleared but with half the effort.

Those who have studied this form of cultivation claim that the soil is richer in humus because the weeds were allowed to go back into it and were not carried away and that it is more fertile because it was not deeply disturbed. Of course, if you have reason to believe that the soil is in poor shape before you plant the crop, you can fertilise or lime the soil first, before weeding it and planting in the manner described.

Having briefly described the current scene, let me return to traditional methods. We dig for several reasons and in several ways. The most important is the autumn preparation of the soil when all empty plots are dug. We then prepare the soil for the coming season. The aim is to get it in a friable condition so that when the time comes to sow seeds in spring we can simply and easily pull the hoe through the soil to make drills for them. At this season we dig in such a way as to leave the elements to do most of the work for us. This varies from the method used during summer when the hot sun bakes the clods of earth into something like bricks, which are often impossible to break down until they have been softened again by rain. If we do dig in summer we should always hack and worry these clods with the tines of a fork until they fall into smaller and smaller pieces. This layer of smaller soil particles on the surface of the soil helps to prevent rapid evaporation of precious moisture from the soil. It forms a dust mulch and those who advocate constant hoeing in summer (I was once one of these) maintain that this is essential to keep moisture in. I say mulching with a moist, humus-making material is better, because it also provides moisture-retentive material for the soil and so increases moisture content in the summer. It is also easier on the muscles – in some ways.

After autumn digging, in most parts of the country and in most years, the soil is almost certain to become frozen from time to time, even if this is no more than ground frost. This has a beneficial effect on the soil and we find that after the ice has thawed and the soil has dried it will crumble nicely. For this reason, when the soil is dug and overturned in autumn, it should not be broken up as it is in summer but left in large, rough clods. No effort should be made to break these down. Nature will do it for you. If you were to leave a nicely levelled plot the winter rains would only flatten and harden it.

But whatever method of soil culture you adopt, do take it easy. Do not attempt to lift too much at one time. Console yourself that slow work is usually neater and better. If you insert your fork, say, 8ins back from the edge of the strip you hope to turn, do realise that you will have continually to lift a mass of soil 8ins thick multiplied by the width and depth of the fork, and this could be quite heavy. Even if you decide to take out a strip only 3ins thick, I think you will be surprised at the progress you make. Try to drive the fork or spade in at right angles to the ground. You will find it helpful whenever and in whatever way you dig, to use some kind of guiding line. If the soil is moist, so much so that it sticks to the soles of your shoes, you should not walk on it, for you will help to destroy its structure. On the other hand it can often be dug in this condition although it is worth remembering that wet soil is so much heavier than dry. The difficulty is that time as well as the day is often short and you feel that you should get on with the digging even if conditions are not perfect. In this case you can use a plank to stand on, and this can also act as a guide line. Never dig frosted soil. If you do, moisture may become locked in and this causes the earth to become waterlogged in spring when it should be dry for best results.

Digging by the traditional method

When you dig, the idea basically is to move the soil from your feet to a spot a little way ahead of you, and as you do so to turn the soil mass upside down so that the top layer, and any small weeds or even mulches, manure or lime spread on it, are buried. The easiest way to dig a plot and to finish up with the soil level is first to cart away all the soil you take from the first row or trench and to deposit this at the end of the plot near where you intend to finish digging. In this way you begin the main digging with a trench made, and you simply fill this trench as you empty the next one. Then, when you reach the end, the soil from the first trench is emptied into it.

Push the fork or spade into the soil vertically, pressing it down with your foot on one side of the main shaft (there are left and right-footed diggers) so that the whole length of the tines or blade is in the ground. Lift the soil mass and as you throw it into the trench directly ahead turn it upside down so that the original soil surface now lies at the bottom of the trench. If you are digging in spring or summer, knock any clods with the fork to break them down, then pass the fork like a comb back and forth to break them down even further, and to level the surface.

This operation is called digging one spit deep and it serves for most purposes. Double digging, or digging two spits deep, consists of digging the bottom of the trench also. One works across the plot from one end to the other, first removing a spit one spit deep and taking the soil from this to the other end of the plot as already described. The trench that is left is then lined with manure or garden compost, and the floor of the trench well worked to incorporate this with the soil. Thus the subsoil is both enriched and aerated. The subsoil, that is the soil below the first spit, should always be kept down below and never brought to the surface.

The next row is then dug one spit deep, the soil from this being thrown into the trench on top of the forked soil. This trench is then lined with the humus-making material you are using and forked to mix it well, and so the process continues until the end of the plot is reached, where the last trench should be enriched and forked and then filled in with the soil brought from the first trench.

Once you have double dug in this way you need not do it again. Perhaps you need not even do it in the first place. It is recommended, however, for heavy or waterlogged soils because it aerates the soil and helps to drain it more quickly. No doubt such soils could be improved by more natural methods but this could well take some years.

It helps also even when you dig only one spit deep, if you incorporate manure, compost or some other humus-making materials as you work. If you have no organic manure, apply a good balanced fertiliser to the soil after it has been dug. You can provide the necessary humus throughout the rest of the year by using peat when you sow or plant, and by mulching between the rows with lawn mownings if this appeals to you, or with rotted compost as it becomes available.

Converting a lawn or uncultivated land

If you are converting a piece of lawn or natural grassland into a vegetable garden, you can either dig in the grass by cutting through the turf as you dig and then upturning it and burying the grass portion under the soil, in which case you should also pull out all tap-rooted weeds such as dandelions as you go, or, you can skim off the grass first. You can do this by cutting through the grass with the edge of a spade, making a series of rectangular cuts and then pushing the spade under the grass to remove a strip of grass or a turf about an inch or two thick to the limits indicated by the spade cuts. These turves can then be neatly stacked, grass side downwards, and left to rot. This will take some months and they will render down into a good loam which you can then use either in potting soil mixtures or planting soil mixtures, or you can simply return it to the soil. Having skimmed the surface of the grass, you then proceed to dig or cultivate the soil beneath in the method which you find most suited to your requirements, your physique or your inclinations.

A short cut I once took with a new plot was to borrow a rotovator and with this to turn up the weedy and uncultivated ground. I found that I could handle the machine quite well for it was a lightweight model, and although the plot is quite a large one it did not take many hours to cover it thoroughly. After turning the soil I spent some time raking up weed roots and burning them, because most perennial roots left in the soil will grow again even if they are sliced or otherwise reduced into small pieces, for they then behave as root cuttings and thus produce more weeds than ever.

Nowadays you can eliminate this task by first going over the plot with Weedol, concentrating on the tough, invasive, perennial weeds such as dock, nettles, hogweed, dandelion, convolvulus and couch grass. Where the weeds are well established and thick it may be necessary to make more than one application of the weedkiller, because although you may kill the green part of the plant above ground, there may be shoots just below the soil, or dormant buds elsewhere which will develop and grow later. Annual weeds such as chickweed, shepherd's purse, groundsel and land cress can be mainly ignored because they will be cut off at the crown by the machine or simply turned into the soil. In either case they will soon die and rot away to make, in effect, what can be described as a green manure.

When you dig you will save yourself considerable time and trouble later if you make provision to collect those weeds you remove from the soil. Keep two containers by you, buckets, boxes, baskets or even bags, one for the perennial roots and one for the leafy tops which you can easily twist off. These tops can help you stock your compost heap.

As I said earlier, there are two schools of thought about digging, and whether or not you continue to dig deeply each year is up to you.

Rotation of crops

Another decision you must make is on the subject of the correct rotation of crops, in other words on vegetable garden planning. There are those who believe and teach that a plot should be divided into three sections, one for leaf and stem crops, one for roots and one for seeds. By following this practice the crops can be rotated each year, one strip being used for each in turn and one third always cleared and double dug each autumn.

I am sure this practice is admirable where there is a large garden staff or some hefty diggers who have lots of time as well as muscle power, and also where a large kitchen garden is concerned. Today's gardens are small and indeed it irritates me that in some of the special demonstration gardens one sees, the paths alone are often as spacious as the average entire kitchen plot. So I do not think the three section method to be really practical for the average garden today. I tried it for years and finally rejected it. Nowadays I would feel that I had failed as a provider if a third of my plot was empty in the winter, and I say this in spite of a well-filled freezer. There is also the point to be considered that tastes are more catholic than they were and crops are more varied today.

My own simpler method is to follow a top crop with a root crop. This is rough and ready I know, but provided that the soil is kept enriched it seems to work well. I imagine that if one's memory is not good, it would help to make a little plan as you go, but as I usually sow or plant a crop immediately following the removal of one, it is not difficult to succeed the one kind with the other.

If you change the location of the very deep penetrating root crops, placing them at one end of the plot one year, in the centre the next and at the other in the third, you will be gaining much the same advantages in a strict rotation. These crops need not necessarily all be in one strip. For instance, there might be three rows of leeks, then a leafy row of some sort, perhaps because it is following a summer root crop, and then parsnips, but all will be roughly concentrated. This method also allows you to plant the roots on ground which has been well enriched for some previous crop.

Clearing the weeds – and hoes

If you mulch the ground thoroughly weeds need not be a constant problem although they will still have to be constantly removed, but you will find that you can do this easily enough. They are more likely to appear in the row itself, among the seedlings, than in the spaces between the rows. Remove them as soon as you see them and always pull out any which you can reach when you are collecting young vegetables such as radish and carrots and when you are down at weeding level anyway. Uprooting a weed seedling causes little disturbance to your crops, but when you have to pull up a larger plant you may draw the others' roots out of the soil too. You can deal with many weeds quite simply by cutting them off at ground level with a knife at such times when you go, for instance, to cut a lettuce. Pull the lettuce plant you want and then simply cut, or in effect hoe, the soil space thus left by the removal of the plant. Quite likely you can reach out a little further and cut down some others. I find this routine practice most helpful and it is surprising how clear of weeds it keeps the crops.

On a larger scale, those weeds which appear between the rows can be smothered by a mulch or they can be cut off with a hoe.

There is more than one type of hoe, most of which have been designed for a special purpose. One which is a good all-rounder and excellent for the beginner is the half-moon shaped draw hoe, which has a swan neck. As its name indicates, you draw it through the ground, skimming the soil surface and cutting through weeds at this point. A hoe is really a chopper on a long handle and correct hoeing entails simply scuffling the soil so that plants are severed from their roots and at the same time the soil surface or crust is broken. Obviously the smaller the plants the easier it is to deal with them, and the quicker they fade and die. You should never waste your precious energy trying to hack the ground with a hoe as though it were a pickaxe. Pull or draw the hoe towards you. This should be a gentle job and you should take care also that you do not cut off any nearby vegetable seedlings. Actually it is best not to use the hoe for some crops, onions for example, in case you damage the bulb, which is usually resting on the soil surface. Hand weed this crop and start doing this as soon as you see the tiniest weed. If you do not disturb the soil you will find that there are not many weed seedlings after the first flux simply because the other seeds remain in the soil, too deep to germinate. Once they are brought up to the surface they will begin to grow.

Two other easy to use hoes are the Saynor and the Push-pull weeder. I find that I use the first more and more. Being quite small in diameter this hoe can easily be passed between growing plants without damaging them. As a soil scuffler I find it perfect and it is also very light in weight. Although it is ideal for cutting through weeds, especially thick ones, the edges of the small irregular oval tool are serrated and I also use it for making shallow drills.

You can also use the swan neck hoe for earthing up potato plants, but if you aim to have several tools I suggest that for this purpose and for general scratching and cultivating of the soil surface, you might consider using a cultivator. This is a three or five pronged tool looking like a claw. I used to use one a great deal before my mulching days and I found it very useful. It had one drawback, it was heavy to use, but perhaps now there are lighter weight models.

Sowing the seed

The swan neck hoe will also serve to cut furrows, or in garden terms, to make drills into which seeds are sown. For this purpose you will also need a rake.

First rake or scratch over the soil to a depth of 2 or 3ins and this way reduce it to a very fine, crumbly texture. This is so that when you draw a drill the soil will be fine and even to its whole depth. Draw the rake back and forth levelling the ground as you go. Do not use the rake to draw all the large particles to one end of the plot as it is so easy to do, but keep moving these backwards and forwards until they crumble and are reduced in size. This is one of the purposes of the rake when used in this way. On the other hand, draw off from the area of soil any debris such as faded weeds, root fibres and stones. The finer or smaller the seeds you are about to sow, the finer should be the soil texture.

If the soil is too dry you can water it gently, but it might often be wise to do this some hours before you are ready to sow the seed, otherwise it might be too sticky. You will get to know in time the best way to treat your individual soil. If you have just one row to sow, put down your line and water just along this so that the soil on which you will have to stand remains quite dry.

Usually you should be able to rake, then lightly tread the soil to firm it and then rake again. By this time it should be easy enough to draw the drills and the soil should be in perfect condition for seed sowing.

Seed must be covered, even if only with the finest sprinkling of soil or peat. You will find directions for the recommended depth on most seed packets and these are also given in the section on specific vegetables further on in this book. A light soil covering ensures that seed is not blown away by wind and that it is not easily spotted and eaten by birds or some other predators. Under the soil it is also kept moist and dark and even warm.

One point that needs watching is that when you make a drill, the soil on either side of the little channel is thrown up and thus makes a miniature bank or wall. Be careful not to fall into the error of taking the top of this as the level of the soil.

Always use a line to guide you when you make a drill. If the plot is narrow you can use your rake handle as a guide. Some people measure and mark a rake handle in foot lengths so they can use it for measuring distances between rows. To make a short seed drill, such as might be required with a small nursery bed in which to raise plants later to be transplanted, lay the rake on the ground so that its back rests flat. Use the angle of the teeth and handle as a set square so that the drills are straight and in line. Take the hoe or the dibber (more of this later) and draw a drill along the side of the rake handle.

It will help you in future if you begin by marking a drill at both ends. Push a stick into the ground at each end of the drill before the seeds are sown. Then, before you draw the next drill, measure the distance required between the rows by means of these guide sticks.

After the seeds have been sown they must be covered with soil. If you know that the soil lacks humus, it is a good plan to use a little moistened peat for the first move in this operation. Go along the drill throwing enough in to hide the seed. Then with the back of the rake, that is, with the flat of it, gently draw the soil from the far side of the drill back over the peat and the seeds. Because the other part of the ridge will still be showing, next level the soil. Probably the best way to do this is to lightly tread along the drill. Remove the line.

The dibber
A dibber is a tool, usually wooden, shaped like the top of a digging fork (indeed, it often *is* the top of a digging fork which was broken at one time) with a pointed end, sometimes shod with metal. It is used for making holes quickly and easily, into which certain plants such as leeks or brassicas are placed. For the latter the dibber is pushed into the soil to the depth of the plant roots. If these are in a good round mass you may need to move the dibber around a little so that the hole is made large enough. Holding the plant with one hand and the dibber in the other, place the plant in the hole, root tip pointing downwards. See that the roots go into the soil at their previous level. You should be able to see the mark on the stem. When the roots are at the same depth as they were, push the dibber in again, this time to the right or left of the hole about an inch or so away from the stem. Then push it down towards the roots and against the plant. This action forces soil into the hole, fills in any large air pockets and anchors the plant. Test this by giving the plant a little tug. It should hold fast. If it doesn't, make another push with the dibber.

If you think that the soil is poor, make a hole a little deeper than necessary, put in some good soil or some peat mixed with a little fertiliser and then insert the plant as suggested above.

Water by filling the second hole made. In time this will become filled with soil.

As I said, dibber planting is quick and easy, but some people prefer to use a trowel. The principle is much the same and you can even firm the roots of a plant the same way by thrusting the trowel into the soil with its back towards the plant.

Planting leeks is even simpler than planting brassicas. In this case you push the dibber down quite deeply, 9ins if possible. Simply drop the leeks one by one into the holes you have made. Water them well, letting the hole fill completely. Nothing else is necessary. The holes gradually fill with soil and the leeks grow with a long portion of the root blanched under the soil.

3

SPACE MAKERS

If you can grow flowering and other ornamental plants then of course you can also grow food plants. If you have not done so because you believe that your garden is too small to accommodate them and still remain attractive, let me assure you that there are likely to be several food crops which you can grow quite well, perhaps even superbly, in a little space. I suggest that it is really a matter of looking at vegetables from a different point of view. If it is not possible to isolate them in a separate plot, then try to see them as interesting garden plants for which you should try to make room and not merely as dowdy tenants of a cabbage patch.

If you would dearly like to try vegetables but are undecided which crops you should attempt to grow, ask yourself which vegetables or herbs would help you most. As some never seem to be in the average greengrocer's shop or supermarket, which scarce types would you like most to be able to have at hand? It might be possible to raise some of these yourself. Which do you find most expensive or which would you use more often if only they were not so dear or so scarce? I suggest that it is on these points that you should plan your crops. Make a list and then eliminate those which obviously, perhaps for climatic reasons, would not fit into your present garden plan, but study them first from all angles before you do this. Check if they *can* be grown in your plot and then *how*. It could be that you will be surprised how very little land would be actually occupied, and even this need not affect the decorative value of your garden. Remember that directions given in seedsmen's catalogues and on seed packets presuppose that everyone will be working on a clear rectangular plot specially set aside for vegetables. This, I suppose, is the case in the majority of gardens and so compromises are not allowed for. So this is an instance where the individual must bend the rules to suit her or his special requirements. If you begin successfully and imaginatively in a small way, you are almost certain to devise other novel ways and means to make room for yet more food plants.

Let me give a few simple examples. How much would it help you to have plenty of garlic and shallots? The first of these is not cheap in the shops, and the second can usually be bought only at one time of the year when the bulbs are sold for pickling. If you like them for cooking it is not possible to buy them all through the year as you can onions, simply because this is not a vegetable demanded by the majority of British cooks. Yet shallots must be quite the easiest of all vegetables to grow. They will keep from one season to the next and they take very little space. They are extremely profitable. From one seed bulb you can expect to lift several ingredients for the kitchen. If you grew nothing else you would not only be making a saving but creating a considerable convenience for yourself. Shallots can be fitted in to many a garden so easily and pleasantly. For instance they could be planted near the edge of a rose bed, somewhere in the sun. As the bulbs are planted in the top inch of soil they will not disturb the rose roots in any way. They need soil which has been well manured, so what goes for the roses will go for them also. If the only place you could fit them in was very much in view, you can pretty them up a little. Bear in mind that they only become shabby in late summer. You could plant some alternate crop with them, parsley perhaps, asparagus peas or simply annual sweet alyssum or some other non-food plant.

Garlic needs to be planted more deeply, 2ins down in good rich soil. The individual cloves should go in in February and be lifted out as compound bulbs in August. Again you lift many for the one you originally planted. As they grow the bulbs make one slender grass-like stem. Surely you could find some space where a few could be grouped in a border where they will get the sun? Once again you can grow something else among them. So long as their tops are in the sun, their bulbs below good soil will look after themselves.

How often can you buy good fresh spinach in winter? Leaf beet or perpetual spinach is handsome enough to be grown in a sheltered border where it will furnish the garden as well as the table. Sow the seed in circular drills among other plants. As it is picked leaf by leaf, the group need never be completely denuded and you can enjoy their splendid splashes of green until you want the plants up and out of the way for spring plantings.

Courgettes make large but neat and handsome plants. You could cut a group of three small beds in the lawn, close together clover-leaf pattern, and grow a plant in each. They will be quite decorative through the summer, for the flowers are large and showy and bloom continuously. If you grow the yellow courgette you will have even more vivid colour than if you grew the plain green. Once these plants are finished you could fill the beds with groups of spring flowers instead, unless you decide to go on with some other decorative vegetables.

And if you have no lawn, why not lift a paving stone or two and grow some plants on the patio or even in the backyard instead? The general appearance of the large palmate leaves and the showy flowers makes this a suitable plant for such a situation. Bush marrows and squash can be grown in this way also and in every case the fruits are decorative. If you want to show off a little (and who doesn't?) grow the orange and red turban-shaped Turk's cap gourd, one of the most delicious when cooked, and the scallop-edged flat custard marrow.

If the children are grown up or are no longer really interested, fill the sand pit with good soil and grow these same plants there, but remember to keep them well watered, because they will in effect be growing in a container. If instead of courgettes, squash or marrows, you fancy cucumbers, grow an outdoor variety. I recommend Suttons egg-sized Apple Cucumber, tender yet crisp, succulent, sweet and burpless, conveniently portion-sized. Either train the long trails up a pillar (they have tendrils but they need a little support to keep them going up in the required direction) or alternatively use them to cover a coal bunker or to clothe a trellis erected around it. This apple cucumber is a handsome plant which becomes smothered with bright little yellow flowers, the females of which develop into the delicious little fruits.

You can grow climbing beans up one side of the house or on each side of the door. Give support to each plant with a string or wire stretched from the ground to the height you want it to reach. You can pinch the tops out when they have reached the height convenient to you. Remember that there are varieties with different colours of bean blossom. Perhaps two friends would join with you to buy a packet each of, say, a white, pink or purple blossomed variety and you could share so that you all have a mixture. Beans have a fairly long season and if they have the protection of a warm house wall you can get them going in May and go on picking from them until the hard autumn frosts. They also look well growing over an arch above a pathway.

If you really are very short of actual soil space in your garden, consider growing some crops in pots which could be ranged along the side of the house, along a garage or shed wall, or even in certain circumstances on a balcony or in a window box. It really can be well worth while. After all, if all you do is to produce enough tomatoes to see you through the summer you will have shown a profit and helped to keep yourself in a little food and so made a tiny contribution to the world food situation. At the same time you will be placing on your table foods which are both more delicious and more vitamin-packed than any you could buy from store or supermarket.

If you do not want or do not have pots it is possible to grow these same crops in special 'Gro Bags' which are marketed by some of the larger garden material or garden chemical suppliers. The large plastic bags contain a well balanced peat mixture with the requisite fertilisers. You merely cut open the bag as directed, plant, water and grow. Splendid crops can be grown this way and some commercial growers are turning to this method as the answer to some of their specialised problems, but the domestic grower must balance the cost of the bags (not inconsiderable) against the savings in bought vegetables and the anticipated crop. The soil mixture in the bags cannot be used again for the same purpose although it can be a useful addition to a garden soil.

These bags can be pushed up against the wall of a house on one side of a path where they will take up little space. I have seen them planted with the crops mentioned above and with lettuce, although I must in all fairness say that this seems to me to be a most expensive method of growing the last crop at a time of year when it can be grown so easily in almost any corner of the garden.

There are many vegetables which can be treated as decorative annuals and grown between flowering plants in herbaceous or annual beds or borders. For instance, if you grow dahlias in a special bed try spacing them wider apart and grow tripods of climbing beans alternately among them. You can vary the colours as I suggested earlier, growing scarlet runners which have scarlet, white or pink blossoms in some groups and the pretty violet flowered and podded climbing French bean variety in another. Sweet corn also grows better in groups or blocks than in rows, because they are then better pollinated, in which case you get lovely completely full cobs. Plant groups of these at the back of a border among the taller flowering perennials. By making the soil rich for them you will be benefiting the border as a whole.

If you prefer it you can actually make a vegetable border in an open sunny site instead of the usual regular rectangular patch hidden away somewhere down at the end of the garden. In my own vegetable plot, which is protected by a large cage of wire netting around the four sides and plastic netting above, there is a mixed border in a south-facing strip 3ft wide at the side of the path. This is raised a few inches from normal ground level. At the moment of writing, at the end of summer, it contains an edging of Remontante strawberries, now fruiting again. Between each of these is a sprouting shallot (see the chapter on Personal Touches) and just behind them are newly planted lettuces to give autumn salads.

Filling the main width of the border there is an assortment of plants, including baby crookneck squash, a non-trailing variety, flanking a stand of tall, feathery asparagus plants which were allowed to grow after producing the spring and early summer crop. The whole border is backed by the wire netting wall of one side of the cage and on this and supported by it are growing runner beans, some of them actually behind the asparagus, and at one end plants of a large fruited golden squash. These plants climb by means of their tendrils but they are also guided and supported in places by the 'Twistem' type of plant tie. Between them these climbers cover the wire netting. By doing so they tone it down so that it is not so obvious from points of view in the flower garden.

After the first frosts, when the climbers are removed and the asparagus cut down, the border will be given a deep mulch of rotted manure, for it is important to keep such a closely planted area in good condition, and it will then carry a crop of winter lettuce and endive. Often, early in the year, early carrots are sown among the remaining plants. As soon as these are ready, it seems, the asparagus will begin to shoot and the strawberries to flower, and after them it is time to sow the beans and squash again.

Although in this case I did not set out originally to make it so, trying simply to use every inch of space, this long border is attractive in its own way and it is certainly always full of interest and very productive.

If your kitchen garden is small, make the most of the little plot by concentrating on small varieties of your favourite vegetables. It is well worth spending some time studying carefully several seed catalogues to discover which these are. For instance, there are dwarf broad beans, and compact lettuce, cabbage, brussels sprouts, sweet corn and French beans.

In the first chapter I remarked that this is not a book advocating or explaining the production of 18in beans or 2lb onions, urging instead the growing and harvesting of small, tasty, nourishing and tender vegetables, quick and easy to cook and sweet on the palate. That these are what most people want is borne out by the fact that hybridists are concentrating on producing quick maturing and compact varieties. This means that more can be grown to the square yard and also that the annual turnover can be increased. If a plant does not have to occupy the soil for as long as it was once expected to, this means that some other crop can occupy that same space more quickly. Thus the value of the garden, physically and financially, is greatly increased.

Couple the quick maturing crops with the added benefit of a deep freezer, which also allows you to clear a mature row at one time instead of a little, day by day, and you increase even further the value of your vegetable garden.

On the other hand, there are some vegetables which we prefer to have waiting our convenience, cabbages and lettuce are particular examples, and it is a nuisance if these grow well beyond their prime before we are ready to crop them. Often one way of getting over this problem is to grow shorter rows in greater succession, and another is to select the modern varieties which are known to be long standing. These keep their compact character and do not bolt or rush to flower and to seed. So if you do not daily consume large quantities of these vegetables, select the long standing types where you can.

It seems to me that the larger the vegetable the more waste in top foliage or outside leaves. True these can go on to the compost heap, but surely it is better to have more, smaller vegetables, and perhaps a greater variety instead? However, whether you space the vegetables according to the measurements demanded by the traditionalists or as stated on the seed packets, or whether like me you decide to grow them closer, is up to you. Do remember though, that the more you grow to the square yard, the more you should feed your soil with good health giving humus as well as more concentrated fertilisers.

Crops are grown so close in my own garden that I often have to tread carefully for fear of damaging some, but I have more to say about this later. In passing, however, I should perhaps say that if ground cover plants are beneficial in a flower garden, where most of us try to cover every inch of soil, then there surely is a role for them to play in a vegetable plot also.

Another way of extending the garden, in the short, dark days at least when fresh green vegetables are either scarce or expensive or both, is to bring it indoors. Whether this is in a greenhouse, conservatory, kitchen or even the spare room doesn't really matter, for there are crops you can grow in all of these places with a minimum of fuss or inconvenience

It is so easy to sprout certain seeds so that they provide crops that can supplement salads, or actually provide an entire dish, as bean shoots do in Chinese cooking. Most vegetable seed leaves and cotyledons make tasty and nutricious eating. You have only to think of mustard and cress, for these two are so easy to grow that you need not hesitate to try them. At one time these were the only kind of sprouting seed you could buy from the seedsmen, but now you can also sprout Mung beans, alfalfa, oats, wheat, rye, millet, fenugreek soybeans and sesame. Some of these, alfalfa for instance, take as little as four days to germinate and be ready for eating. According to the quantity you require (and for the greatest value it is usually best to sow the crops to give you a succession) you can grow them as children do on moist tissue, flannel or some other cloth held in a saucer or in one of those plastic trays supermarket food often comes packed in, or in jars, or like they do in some Chinese restaurants, in buckets.

Then there is forcing, again quite easy. You can, for example, force chicory in pots or in black plastic bags in any warm place indoors, even in the cupboard under the sink!

4

A WARM SOIL GIVES BETTER, EARLIER VEGETABLES

It is comforting to think that if you improve the texture of your soil you will also make it a warmer soil and the warmer and better drained it is the better crops it will carry in winter. It is possible so to plan these crops that they will grow in the open, but by providing some means of protection for them you can add to their variety and even grow other crops which are normally too tender to stand the expected rigours of the winter months.

General protection
Obviously the more shelter you can provide the warmer the garden will be, and this is why in so many of the old large private gardens the kitchen garden was walled around, and the choicest fruit placed against the warm south and west facing walls.

I am not suggesting that a wall on the coldest side of the vegetable plot is essential, but since so many people replan a garden in order to fit in a kitchen plot conveniently and unobtrusively, I am suggesting that at this time it might be possible to build a wall. Even one of the attractive open-work pierced screen walls would provide valuable protection. Most frequently people plant a hedge to establish a boundary, but this is not always wise in proximity to the vegetable growing area, for often hedging plants rob the soil quite considerably and this is something that should be taken seriously into account. It is worth bearing in mind that even a wire netting screen will ward off a mild frost and also help to soften the bitterness and strength of a strong or persistent wind. If you wish, you can add to the value of a wire netting fence by using it to support some fan trained or espalier trees. These could rise from a narrow border in which you can also grow some of the smaller vegetables such as lettuce, or perhaps some herbs.

My own vegetable garden is enclosed in a wire netting cage, and I am often surprised how much warmer it is inside this than outside. However, additional protection has also been provided. On the north side is a herb bank, not a border. In this the soil is raised in a long mound and the top becomes a little higher each year as mulches and peat are slowly added to it. The plants which grow on the bank also had height and as some of these are tall fennel, melissa and apple mint, there are times when the fence or wall thus made is some eight feet tall in places. This feature, as you can imagine, provides considerable protection from the north and helps to trap the sun's heat in the caged area. On the east is another barrier, made not only to protect the garden but also to screen its utilitarian appearance from the house. This consists of a peat hill on which grow a number of calcifuges or lime haters, heathers, rhododendrons, azaleas and the like. Thus the kitchen garden is in effect walled or protected on two of its coldest sides and open to the south and the west. The rows of vegetables run from north to south, so each row gets the maximum of the available sunlight. All along the north side of this cage, facing south and backed by the herb bank, runs the narrow raised border I mention in the chapter on Space Makers.

Cloches

In spite of the protection thus given by simple landscaping, even more is provided in the form of cloches. I use Novolux plastic cloches, light, transparent, strong and durable, instead of glass which I found was constantly being broken, a factor which increased expense and formed a constant hazard. These plastic cloches come in a flat pack which is normally on sale in any garden centre. The kit consists of a fairly rigid though pliable rectangle of corrugated plastic complete with two galvanised wire hoops fitted with legs and a smooth plastic sheet for closing the ends. The corrugated plastic sheet is curved and a hoop is slid over it at each end. The wire extension which forms the legs is then pushed into the soil, where they anchor the cloches firmly. The lower edge of the plastic rests on the soil and when ventilation is necessary one simply raises the cloche away from the soil so that a current of air is created in the interior. The ends of the cloche are sealed by fixing the rectangle of plastic close against it and holding it there by pushing a cane into the soil on each side so that it rests against the plastic and holds it in place. You can push the cloches next to each other so that they form in effect a continuous tunnel.

It is possible to buy a cheaper type of tunnel cloche particularly suited to larger areas of vegetables, probably even on a commercial scale. In this case the plastic is in thinner sheeting or film and in long strips. It is placed over galvanised wire hoops, pulled taut and firmly fastened at the ends so that it is not caught by the wind. This type of cloche is really most effective, but it is a little more fiddling when you come to harvest your crops unless you are clearing an entire row at one time. A Novolux cloche is so easily lifted, moved aside and replaced when you have done what you wish.

In my opinion it really is worth while investing in some cloches. Even if you can afford no more than one or two to begin with, this still means that you can, say, protect portions of a row of winter lettuce, or a mixed row, and as the portion under the cloche is cut you can move it along the row until in time all have been covered at some time. If you have sufficient cloches to stretch along the entire plot so much the better. You can plan your winter crops so that one cloche covers a stretch of two or three different kinds growing in rows near each other. In this case you need to sow the tallest kind at the centre with a short kind on each side. Or there are other methods, as I describe in the chapter on Personal Touches.

After having protected the crops in winter and early spring, you can make further use of the cloches to warm and even slightly to dry any empty soil you have, so that you can make an early start with those crops that do best if they are sown early in the season. The cloches need not be left over these for long. Usually once they are showing through the ground they can be left to get on with growing naturally if you need the cloches elsewhere. So you can see what a versatile aid these cloches can be.

You can steal a march in many ways. If you like really early crops of broad beans and round peas, both of which can be sown in November, you can help these considerably by covering them with cloches, and as I said earlier, you can tuck something else in along with them to save wasting all the under-cloche space.

Cloches can be placed over the first crop of early potatoes. It is worth growing just one row this way so as to protect them from frost and help them to produce tubers at the time when new potatoes are at their most expensive. If you begin sprouting them early, as described in the relevant section, you can often dig them by the end of May. Dwarf French beans sown in April under cloches will give you beans in early summer. You can cover all those vegetables that you consider to be real summer kinds and that you are impatient to eat while they are young and tender, such as peas, carrots, radish and lettuce.

Later in the spring the cloches can be used to provide the essential soil and air warmth to cucumbers and other members of the marrow family, to sweet corn, runner beans, and outdoor tomatoes, and any other tender crop you might wish to grow and harvest.

In a cool summer you can continue using them as a protection for these same plants, rather in the manner that people use a windbreak on the sand at some of our brisker resorts. Stand the cloches on end so that they partly encircle the plants inside, so trapping what little sun there may be, or place them at one side to protect them from the prevailing wind. In this case the cloches can be anchored by using canes. Push one through the loops in the centre of the two wire hoops which encircle the cloches, and then push or hammer the cane firmly into the soil.

In early autumn you can place the cloches over late or reluctant-to-ripen fruits of melons, marrows and others so as to give them additional warmth. If the nights become cold, cloches placed over late summer sown French beans, dwarf peas, beetroot and lettuce will help them to mature more quickly so that you get full value from them.

In a very small garden, cloches placed in a warm sheltered spot can often serve the same purpose as a cold frame. On the other hand, a frame placed away from the actual vegetable garden can help to extend it, for it can be used for several purposes. It can be used as a nursery for seedlings, and in this case it is usually most helpful to sow these in boxes or pots so that they may easily be moved on to make room for more as soon as they are ready for transplanting. It can be used to harden off those plants which have been raised in greater warmth before they are set out in open ground, including such plants as those of the marrow family, French and runner beans, tomatoes, sweet corn and other half-hardy kinds. It can also be used to house lettuce, endive, carrots and mustard and cress through winter and in early spring. Obviously, if you hope to do all of these things one small frame will not be sufficient, and this is why I suggest that cloches and a warm soil might be more practical for most small gardens.

The cold frame

A cold frame is one which is not heated in any way, although we have seen that leaves and hot beds can be used to generate heat. It is possible to have electric heat in a frame (see below), and as you would expect, if you site a frame in a sunny, sheltered spot it will keep warmer for longer than if it is in a cold place. A cold frame is quite satisfactory to raise seedlings of brussels sprouts, broccoli, cauliflowers, leeks, lettuces, onions, peas, and broad beans sown in February and March, in which case they will be more forward than any which would be sown outdoors. The more tender kinds such as cucumbers and members of the marrow family, French and runner beans, sweet corn, tomatoes and others cannot be sown in frames before April unless the frame is heated in some way. Often it is better to raise these indoors, on a sunny windowsill for example, and then transfer them to frames when they are forward enough. Here they can be hardened off, that is, given more and more ventilation until the frosts have passed when they can go into the open.

As with cloches it is possible to grow certain crops from seed to maturity in a frame, but if you plan to do so you should realise that the frame cannot be used for any other purpose during this time. So-called winter crops, which include young carrots, mustard and cress, lettuce, endive, corn salad, and radish, occupy the frame from the end of September to mid-March, which means that the frame cannot be used to raise seedlings in early spring. All of these crops can be grown quite well under cloches. In summer the frame can be used for tomatoes and cucumbers, but here again there are now such good hardy varieties that both of these can be grown outdoors with less trouble, so if you think that you have really no room, nor the desire for a garden frame, you can most certainly manage without.

Frames vary considerably. It is possible to make a small one simply by using the four sides of a wooden box and placing a pane of glass or a piece of clear plastic on top. The standard frame measures 6ft by 4ft. Two or three of these placed along the wall of a garage, greenhouse or some similar structure would, as you can appreciate, provide a good area in which to grow vegetables, even if this was for only a part of their life.

The shape and style of a frame can also vary. A row such as I have just mentioned, against a wall, would be lean-to. There are also some which have span roofs. A lean-to frame can slope from as much as 3ft at the back to 9 or 7ins in the front. The lights, as they are called, are sloped so as to catch the greatest possible amount of light. Plants grown inside the frames must be as near to the lights as possible, but they must not press against the glass or they will scorch.

A frame can have wooden, brick, or concrete walls, and the best kinds are those which are only a little higher at the back than they are at the front, say a 6in fall from back to front for a 6ft light. It is important if you install frames that you have the kind that you can move easily by yourself without having to go and look for help. Before making or buying frames study catalogues and go and see some on show so that you can decide which will suit you best.

Warming the frame electrically

Many makers or suppliers of frames will also sell the necessary apparatus for warming them by electricity. If you have a conveniently close supply of electricity there is no doubt that soil warming by electric cables will make your frame an invaluable piece of gardening equipment. But if you have to bring your supply for some distance, making use of the special armoured cable that is normally necessary, it may be that the cost will be prohibitive. In this case it may even be worth while to erect one or two frames beside the house or the garage to take advantage of a nearby and convenient electricity supply, even though by doing this you will be splitting your vegetable raising plot into two.

The presence of live electricity cables immediately below the surface of the soil in which you are working with a metal spade or trowel can have a somewhat inhibiting influence on the nervous, but safety is in-built and so far as I am aware there has been no recorded case of any untoward accident with heating of this type. The special heating wires or cables are heavily insulated, sometimes armoured and always perfectly safe even when joined to a mains voltage supply. It is more usual, however, for amateur fixtures to be run through a transformer which reduces the voltage to about 12 volts, which is so low that it can cause no possible harm.

These heating wires are laid in parallel rows some 4–6ins below the soil surface and the loading will depend on the temperature required. As a general average 6 watts per square foot is sufficient for most crops, and the loading for the entire frame will then be worked out on the basis of the area times 6. The normal 6ft by 4ft frame will have an area of 24 sq ft and require a heating element capable of giving 144 watts. The soil warming units are usually switched on according to automatic timers for 10 to 12hrs per night, possibly at intermittent intervals. A thermostat can be fitted if required to ensure that the temperature is never allowed to fall below a certain required figure.

But soil warming is not the only means of heating a frame, it is also possible to fit warming cables or tubes to the sides to warm the air instead of the soil direct. As a rule soil warming will be found to be the more efficient means for general purposes and probably less costly than air warming as the soil will tend to hold and maintain the warmth it receives for longer periods than the air.

Seed raising in plastic bags
So far as seed raising is concerned, many of the half-hardy subjects such as cucumbers and other members of the marrow family, tomatoes and sweet corn have to be raised in warmth. Those who have no greenhouses and no propagating cases may wonder how best to do this. Even the little and inexpensive propagating cases hold so few seeds that they can be only of limited value to the home gardener. I find that the safest way is to sow the seed, either individually in pots or in seed pans or boxes and then to envelope the filled container in a transparent plastic bag.

There are a few points which should be observed. Use a good seed sowing compost such as a John Innes mixture or one of the soil-less kinds such as Levington marketed by Fisons or Kerimure by ICI. Almost fill the container with the slightly moistened compost, then sow the seed, cover it lightly with more compost and water it carefully. Allow surplus water to drain away. Select bags which will be large enough to take the filled seed container, or perhaps to take three or four in a group, leaving enough space at the top to accommodate the seedling plant when it grows.

Inflate each bag and fasten the top securely so that it is airtight. You can stand the package near a radiator, in an airing cupboard or even peg it up over a stove and it will come to no harm. The soil will not dry out because evaporation cannot take place except inside the sealed bag, which must be kept tightly closed. If it is apparent that condensation on the inside of the bag is excessive, open the bag and take out the seed box or pot. Turn the bag inside out and replace and re-seal.

The moment you can see that the seeds have germinated, the packages should be stood in daylight, preferably on a window sill and as near to the light as possible. If this is not done the seedlings will become drawn and spoiled.

Usually, when germination takes place more condensation appears on the inside of the bag and if once again this is worrying, turn the bag inside out.

The plants can remain in the bags until they are crowding it. It is wise to let them stay inside if the nights are cold and they are near the glass of the window. On no account should the leaves rest against the sides of the bags or they will be liable to scorch in sunlight. If necessary move them to larger bags. Repotted plants are also likely to need larger bags. Before hardening off the plants, introduce them to the outer air indoors. First undo the bags, opening the tops wide for a day or two, and then gradually turn them down until they reach the rims of the pots, pans or boxes. This same method can be used in a cold frame or greenhouse.

5

ABC OF VEGETABLES

Artichoke, Jerusalem

Soil preference, good, rich but rather dry. Tubers are ready for eating any time after the foliage begins to turn colour. They are best left in the soil and lifted as required, because they tend to shrivel and become dry in store, and when this happens they are difficult to prepare for the table. Leave a few inches of cut stem showing so that you can easily find the tubers when you go to dig for them.

There are two types of tuber, the old round purple or white and the newer French variety, Fuseau, which has long tubers and a better flavour. If you cannot buy the seed tubers from a garden centre or shop, those you buy from a greengrocer for eating should be suitable for planting too. After this beginning, simply set aside your own tubers for seed.

Plant in February or March, the earlier the better, 18ins apart. If you have more than one row, set them 3ft apart.

The tubers tend to become invasive, so grow this crop some place where it can have room to itself.

Asparagus

One could not honestly list this as a vegetable for beginners to grow if one insisted that it should be grown only in the traditional manner. For various reasons, not least the one concerning space (asparagus beds and the alleys are very wide), I decided to try some other way of raising a few plants so that we could have at least a taste or two when the spears were at their most expensive. You will not get such large crops by using the methods I employ, but I can promise that you will cut enough to gladden your heart!

You will, of course, have to be very patient. It is important not to pick any spears the first year after planting and it is best to wait three years. However, once established the plants will go on for 20 years or more.

Keep in mind the fact that an asparagus plant grows very tall and wide by the end of summer and allow space for this. Picking should cease at about midsummer and after this time the spears which develop will grow 4 or 5ft tall, perhaps more, and will become very bushy, so much so that they are best staked or they will become a nuisance.

In the chapter on Space Makers I described the narrow raised bed in my own garden where asparagus and other plants grow. Instead of following the traditional method of making a 9in deep and 9in wide trench for the plants, I planted each one in individually dug holes, although I followed much the same method otherwise as recommended for trenches. It is as follows: Place a line along the bed and with canes mark the stations where the crowns are to be planted, at least 15ins apart. (Take into consideration the width of the hole when planting.) Remove the soil at each place so that you take out a hole roughly 9ins square. Prepare some good soil, mix it with some nicely rotted compost, or if you have none of this with some balanced fertiliser. You need enough to make a little mound about 4ins high at the bottom of each hole and sufficient to cover each crown as well. Keep the crowns wrapped until you are ready to plant them. Take them out one at a time and spread the string-like roots out and down over the mounds with the centre of the crown at the apex. Cover the roots immediately with some more of the special soil. It is important that the roots do not dry out. Then replace the soil you dug out. This should cover the crown with about 4 or 5ins. Firm the soil by treading it lightly. Leave the canes in to mark the sites.

If you buy your asparagus roots from a seedsman or specialist they will have to be posted to you. They will travel safely enough, but do realise that they should be planted without delay. Have the sites prepared and soil mixed so that you can simply unpack and plant the roots immediately they come into your hands.

After planting it is important to keep the bed clear of weeds. If you wish you can grow some catch crop on the margins of the raised bed as I have indicated elsewhere. I have an edging of Remontante strawberries along mine as well. The important thing to keep in mind is to avoid growing those catch crops which cause the soil to be much disturbed, for asparagus roots grow very near the surface. Lettuce, carrots, turnips, dwarf beans, corn salad and land cress are good catch crops for this purpose so long as they are pulled or cut when young and tender. When I sow seed among and in front of the plants I mix it with plenty of good soil and scatter this on the surface instead of making drills.

Let the spears grow tall and feathery and then wait until the foliage turns yellow before you cut the plants down to about an inch or so above ground level. This is the time to apply a good mulch of well-rotted manure or compost and it helps also to apply some long-lasting basic slag at a rate of roughly ½lb to a 30ft bed. If you have some wood ashes you can dust the plant spaces with a little in early spring, or alternatively apply a ½oz of sulphate of potash to each plant. It helps in March to apply some nitrogenous fertiliser such as nitrochalk, about a teaspoonful to a plant. Repeat this routine every year.

When you are ready to pick the spears, wait until they are about 3ins above the soil. Cut them by pushing a sharp knife, a true asparagus knife if you can get one, obliquely into the soil at the side of the shoot, cutting it some 4ins below the surface. You have to take care when you do this that you do not damage others growing below the soil.

Aubergines

Recently I have been pleasantly surprised to learn how many people I know are now growing these vegetables, for so long considered for epicures and in the luxury class only. Perhaps their new found popularity is due to the fact that the seed hybridists have been busy among these plants and have now produced varieties which are within the scope of the average gardener. Short Tom, which matures much more quickly than the usual type, is an example. Or is it that we are becoming more daring gardeners?

The thing to bear in mind is that this is a tropical plant and so needs as much warmth and protection as you can give it.

One word of warning, where tomatoes for example quickly show that the flowers have set, aubergines take a longer time and they swell more slowly, so do not assume that the plants are not fruiting because the fruits are not at first obvious. They take about 4–5 months to mature. If you are in a cool area you may need to take the plants indoors, or to protect them with a cloche at the end of summer.

So long as you sow the seed in warmth and continue to grow the seedlings in a warm place they should be all right. Aim for temperatures of between 13–20°C (55–65°F) or even a little higher until the plants are about 3ins high. They are also a good crop for the cold greenhouse, a conservatory, garden room, or if you have a suitable one, for a wide sunny window sill. However, indoors you have to strike the balance between not providing too much humidity yet not keeping the atmosphere so dry that the plants are attacked by the red spider mite which thrives in hot, arid conditions. Bear in mind also that seedlings do not like to be too wet or they may damp off.

The seeds are large enough to handle individually, so sow them singly in small pots. Move them when they fill these, usually when they are about 3ins high, to large pots, the larger the better, more than 6ins diameter. At this time also insert a stake, a stout cane, for later use. By inserting it at this stage you will not injure roots. Use a good, rich potting compost. I half-filled my own pots with rotted animal manure and topped this with John Innes Potting Compost. You can also mix your own potting compost, using three parts good loam to one part peat with the addition of one 5in flower pot full of bonemeal to each bushel of the mixture.

The plants need plenty of water once they begin growing fast. When they are about 6ins tall, top them, i.e., pinch out the growing tip, and then tie the main stem to the cane. You may need to support other stems later if they are heavy with fruit.

I feed my aubergines with the same food, and at the same times and intervals, as I feed the tomatoes near them. Do not be tempted to leave too many flowers on the plants, but limit each to about six fruits, or four if you wish them to grow really large.

Broad beans

These are really obliging and generally tough and hardy vegetables. According to where you live or the degree of shelter you have in the garden, you can sow the seed in late October or November, in January or February or in March, like many other vegetables. And if you have missed the first sowings, or perhaps have such a passion for these vegetables that you want more, you can sow them in April or the beginning of June so as to have more in late summer and early autumn. I remember when I was a girl that so many of our neighbours used to lift a row of early potatoes in June and then sow broad beans immediately in the cleaned, newly turned-over soil. Often these people were still picking the beans in October.

As I remarked earlier, these are plants that will take the wind, so they are good to grow right across the plot as a protection for more tender types. If you do this and grow the tall varieties, be sure to grow a double or even a treble row. Even so it might be necessary to stake them against the wind. When they are 12 to 18ins high drive in two stout stakes at each end of the row, a little over the width of the row apart. Tie stout string, or fix wire along each side of the row to reach the tops of the plants. They will then be well supported as they grow taller.

If you think that your garden is sheltered enough for you to chance a November sowing, you should also ensure that the soil is light as well as rich. The later crops, February and March sown, will tolerate heavier soil, indeed broad beans like fairly heavy soil so long as it is well drained and not wet and cold. But heavy soil will not carry seed through the cold, wet days, as I know to my cost on clay, and I had failures when I used to try the November sowing system. Mice also helped to reduce the number of seeds which germinated. You can of course use cloches, and if you do I suggest that you sow one of the dwarf varieties such as The Midget, for this will not push up against the top of the cloche by spring as the taller varieties undoubtedly will. Some varieties are better than others for autumn sowings. Aquadulce, otherwise called Giant Seville, is the most popular variety for this purpose.

Broad beans are usually sown in double rows with a 6in space between to serve as one thick row. If you grow more than one of these, space the other double row about 2ft away or one will overshadow the other. Apart from anything else you will need room to walk through the rows when you pick the beans. If you are short of space you can sow a catch crop of lettuce, brassica seedlings or radish between them to use the ground until the bean plants grow taller.

Sow the seeds Tom Tiddler fashion, that is to say alternately in their rows, so that seeds in one row face the gaps between the seeds in the other.

The Midget and similar dwarf varieties need to be sown only in single rows because their habit of growth is much bushier than others. Good plants of this type should grow to about 18ins through and 12 to 15ins high. The taller varieties grow to 3ft and higher. However, these little beans do not produce such long pods nor such large seeds as the tall varieties, although personally I think that they are much more tender. I certainly find them very convenient, neat garden plants.

Seed is usually sold by the pint or half pint and a half pint contains about 100 seeds, so this should sow a double row of some 25ft if the seeds are sown about 6 to 9ins apart. They should be sown about 2–3ins deep and I think that you will find it easier to dibble these in or to plant them with a trowel than to draw out a drill. If you have a few seeds left over, plant them in a little group at the end of the row. You can then transplant them later should you find any gaps in the rows.

The growing tips of the tall varieties should be nipped out when they are in full flower. This has the effect of filling the pods which then quickly form, and also of deterring attacks of blackfly. The dwarf varieties need not be pinched out. One of the best ways of keeping down blackfly is to save some water from the weekly wash and regularly pour this over the plants, using either a syringe or a fine rose on a watering can. You can also use derris dust, harmless to humans or some of the more powerful poisons such as malathion. But always check labels before you use any of these and make sure particularly how long you must wait before collecting a crop.

You may notice that while you still have mature beans, new growth begins to appear at the base, often showing flower buds. It is possible to cut off the old growth and to allow these others to mature, but personally I have never found this really worth while. When you look at the width of the ground such a row occupies and you measure the very small crop of beans that these late flowers produce, you are sure to appreciate that this space could be more profitably used. If space is no object then no doubt a few beans in autumn, however few, will not come amiss. So unless the latter is the case grub out each plant as it finishes fruiting and use the land for something else as quickly as possible.

In a previous chapter I suggested that a frame could be used to give many vegetables a good start as well as for actually raising some crops. This applies to broad beans. In order to give beans a good start, especially in cold districts, sow the seeds in deep boxes or pots in February in a heated greenhouse or a sunny window sill, or alternatively in a warm frame in March. These plants should then be gradually hardened off and planted outdoors in about mid-April unless weather conditions are poor, in which case you might be wise to wait a little longer. Dwarf varieties can be grown in a soil-warmed frame. Sow them 6ins apart in the warm soil in December or January. Alternatively sow 4 or 5 seeds to a large pot and then plunge the pots in the warm soil up to their rims. From then on see that they do not become dry and give the plants plenty of ventilation. Although they need the warmth around their roots they should not be coddled.

French beans

In French cooking these beans are called 'Haricots', or more likely, 'Haricots vert'. In England they are more generally called French beans or kidney beans, the latter because the seeds are kidney shaped. However, not all French beans have kidney-shaped seed. For instance, the so-called pea-beans are simply French beans that have round seeds. In Britain for some reason the term 'haricots' has become applied to the dried seeds or pulses taken from the ripened pods of certain varieties, the white seeded types of French bean. Some varieties provide better haricots than others. To avoid confusion it will be to these, the dried white seeds, that I refer when I write of haricots. To explain further, since I have found that some confusion does exist between old hands as well as new gardeners, these beans are also known in cooking as flageolets, a term which is applied to the seed of any shelled bean which might be white and dried, or according to variety, brown, black, red, robin-egg speckled, yellow, jade or simply mottled. To be flageolets these need not be dried. Some beans are shelled like peas when the seeds become large enough, simply because people prefer the seed to the pod. If you should go away on holiday and come back to find all your beans 'old', simply shell them and eat them as flageolets.

These are wonderful plants for all gardeners and in particular for those with small gardens. I was enchanted recently when a young and very new gardener told me, 'They are such lovely little plants, so neat. I always thought that beans were so complicated – all those poles! And there are at least fifty beans to a plant!'

He is right. The dwarf varieties of French beans *are* neat and prolific and very little trouble. Yet there are also some climbing varieties, among which the purple-podded Blue Coco is, in my opinion, unsurpassable. The pods turn green when cooked and are succulent enough to be described as almost buttery. One great advantage that French beans have over runners is that they are ready for picking earlier. Generally speaking, French beans take 14, runners 16 weeks to mature from the time of sowing.

The only time these particular vegetables are likely to cause anxiety or to give you a little extra trouble is when they are germinating. They need a high germination temperature. When they are planted too early in open ground during a cold spring they simply lie in the soil until they rot or until they are found and eaten by mice. This is why it is often best to start them off in warmth. If you live in the north or in a cold district I suggest that if you have no cloches but have to sow them indoors instead, that you sow them individually in divided seed containers or in soil blocks. Use any good loam for this instead of special soil composts which can come rather expensive for this purpose. You will then find that the roots are little disturbed when the beans are transplanted into the open ground, and consequently the growth of the plants is not badly checked. This reluctance to germinate in cold soil is one of the reasons why plants from late July sowings do so well. So be patient. Unless you can provide them with some means of warmth, wait until the kinder weather comes before sowing them outdoors. As you would expect, the best French beans are grown in the most sheltered spots.

If you have cloches and if you can make the soil warm by adding plenty of compost or peat or well rotted manure, you can sow them as early as mid-March in the south and a week or two later as you go further north, but personally I think that it is safer to wait until the latter half of April wherever you are. Recommended times for sowing in the open are the end of April, middle of May, beginning of June and the end of July. The last may need cloche protection in early autumn. If you intend to grow haricots, then obviously you should plan to give the plants as long a period in which to mature and ripen as possible. So get them in early. They have to be lifted when the pods turn brown, usually in September.

Beans do not like an acid soil although they do like it rich and well manured. If you know your soil is a little on the acid side dust it with lime before sowing or planting.

It is not wise to count on every bean germinating because only about three out of every four do this. Although the recommended distance apart for these plants is 6ins, I suggest that you sow them 3ins apart and later remove some plants so that you will have a row in which all are 6ins apart. If you do this when the soil is moist so that you can lift a good root ball, you will be able to transplant the thinnings or pass them on to a neighbour. Carry out this operation when three leaves are formed. Any transplants will come into production later than the row of undisturbed plants, so in this way you can ensure a useful succession. Sow the seed 2ins deep and if you have the patience with the little scar downwards against the soil. It is from this point that the root will emerge and one assumes that the roots will get going quicker if they do not have to work their way around the seeds to point downwards.

For those who have small gardens I would like to stress that there is no need to plant French beans in rows. These are plants you can grow in little groups so long as this will not make it difficult for you to pick easily from each plant. Two dozen plants will provide you with many pickings for at least a month to five weeks by successional sowings or plantings. You should be able to pick French beans from June to October.

If the weather is dry and you wonder if the summer-sown beans will germinate quickly enough, you can water the drills before sowing the seeds. I once read that you should on no account soak the seeds, but in fact I had already done just that. It was during a period of a prolonged drought and I soaked the beans for two hours. All I can say is that I never had anything germinate quite so quickly, nor continue to grow so well. The plants were well mulched and I continued to water them thoroughly as they grew.

It is always a good plan to water the plants with a liquid manure when the pods form. It is not essential but it does help to promote heavy crops of beans and to keep the plants in bloom.

Haricot beans can be dual purpose, for you can pick them green as well as allowing them to dry. I suggest that if you have only the one row of only one variety of haricot, that you pick green beans from alternate plants and leave every other one to ripen. These are not beans for successional sowings.

You will find them specially listed in seed catalogues. I recommend Comtesse de Chambord, which has been popular for many years. A newer variety is Carters Granda.

When the pods turn brown, wait until all are ripe and then lift the plants on a dry day and hang them heads downward somewhere where they will continue to dry thoroughly, in a shed or garage for instance. When the leaves on the plants have shrivelled and are brittle to the touch you will know that the beans inside the pods are dry enough to be shelled. A word of warning! Do not be in too much of a hurry to shell the beans. While they are inside the pods they are hermetically sealed, safe and sterile. If the plants are not in your way and so long as they are in a dry atmosphere, you can leave them where they are for some weeks. Shelled beans are best stored in airtight jars.

Runner beans

'A single packet of seed gives you pounds and pounds of fresh, tasty beans at the most welcome time of late summer. As a bonus, the quick growing plants make pleasant garden screens.' From Dobies catalogue, 1975.

Generally the claim in the first sentence is a true one, but in the hot dry summer of that same year many gardeners had bean plants, even those that made pleasant garden screens, smothered with brilliant flowers of which none or only a handful made pods. Meanwhile the dwarf and climbing French beans were doing magnificently. This really is an unusual occurrence. In normal years runner beans are produced so generously that the gardener is often at his or her wits end looking for ways of using or preserving them. Once we could only pack them in layers of salt in jars. Now, of course, one stores them comparatively easily in the freezer. Seed catalogues indicate the best varieties for freezing.

These beans will grow in any good garden soil but they will do best where this is deep and well manured. It is possible to grow beans in the same place year after year, which is convenient since most of us have one place which is more suitable than any other.

Runner beans are coarser than French beans and they do not vary quite so much between themselves, although modern varieties do seem to be leaning a little towards the qualities we find in the French beans. The White Stringless, for example, has white flowers, white seeds and no strings to be removed before slicing or snapping, although it does have the rougher skin of the runner bean.

One used to be able to buy the large white-seeded bean, The Czar, which could be dried and used as a large butter bean, but this seems now to have vanished from the seedsmen's lists for some reason or other.

If you particularly like runner beans but do not wish to become involved in the business of staking the plants, you can grow a non-climbing variety such as Hammonds Dwarf Scarlet. This matures early and is a heavy cropper. Personally I find it irritating because the beans are so often sickle shaped and difficult to string, even by using a potato peeler.

As beans like soil in which there is a great deal of organic matter (although they do not like an acid soil) many gardeners spend the winter and early spring months preparing a trench for them which contains at least 3ins of manure topped with some 6ins of good soil. However, if you are in the habit of mulching rather than digging, you can simply cover the soil with well-rotted manure, and then, should you think it necessary, you can feed the plants when they are beginning to make pods.

Runner beans like sunshine, so don't try to grow them in a shady part of the garden. Partial shade at a brief period of the day will do them no harm. As they are climbing plants they should be encouraged to grow upwards. This also ensures that the bean pods will hang downwards and grow straight. If the plants were not supported and instead allowed to sprawl and spread over the surface of the ground the pods would grow crooked. They would also become soiled and eaten by slugs and insects.

There are several ways of supporting the plants. That which is the easiest and which in the end really takes least space is to grow the plants up tripods of three or five canes (a support to each plant) or poles firmly driven into the ground and securely lashed together at the top. If you grow the beans in long rows, usually the beans are planted in a double line and the poles on each side are then inclined towards each other and joined at the centre above the space between the rows to make a tent-like structure. Alternatively, strong twine can be used instead of poles, but you should remember that the plants are likely to be very heavy when they are carrying a full crop. To use the twine method drive a stout post in at each end of the row to reach about 6ft tall. A length of wire should be tightly stretched between the posts some 6ins from the ground and another 5ft 6in from the ground. Then above each plant twine should be tied from wire to wire. The vines can then climb the lengths of twine. The shoots should be pinched out from the plants when they reach the top wire. If you think that twine will not be strong enough, you can tie canes between the two wires. You can also buy a special kind of netting to support beans and as I have described elsewhere, you can always grow them up a wire netting screen.

The seeds can be sown in the open ground or individually in small pots or other containers and then planted out. Generally the first week in May is considered to be a good time for this first outdoor sowing, and at this time they should be sown 3ins deep, 4ins apart. If you have prepared a special strip of ground for them and well manured it, the soil here should be comparatively warm. See my remarks on this subject in the chapter on Personal Touches. There is no need to make drills, simply dibble the seeds in using a garden line as a guide.

After May the seed need not be sown quite so deeply, 2ins should be sufficient. You gain little by sowing them in the open ground too early unless you can give them cloche protection. I have sown these beans as late as July. Generally the seeds germinate in 10–12 days, although I have had soaked beans which appear a week after sowing in a hot season. If you sow them outdoors without cloches, time this operation. You should be able to estimate when the seeds will appear above the soil without being caught by frost. When two good leaves are formed, thin out to 8ins apart.

You can make sure of an early crop of beans by sowing seed in boxes or pots early in May or at the end of April. I recommend that you sow them individually rather than en masse in a box simply because less root damage is caused. However, if you do use a box and have no frame, fill it two-thirds full of soil that is not too dry. Sow the beans 2ins apart each way and cover with about 1in of soil. Place a pane of glass or a sheet of plastic over the top of the box and keep it in a warm but not hot place. The box can be placed out of doors during the day so long as it is protected at night or taken indoors if there is fear of frost.

After the seeds have germinated and the young leaves start to expand, water the plants as the soil becomes dry. On the first of June, or earlier if it seems likely that there will be no frost, transplant the beans to their permanent quarters, placing them in a row or group with about 8ins between each plant.

If you use the seed box method (and by the way you will need deep boxes and not the usual seed trays) do lift the plants very carefully so that you do not check them. Before transplanting always make sure that the soil in the box is moist. Dry soil will fall away from the roots taking precious rootlets and root hairs with it. Treat plants individually grown in pots in the same way.

Use a small hand fork to lift the plants from the box. It is usually best to remove a plant from the corner of the box first. If you take out the roughly rectangular area of soil surrounding this plant, the space left will leave you room to lift the other plants easily. You should be able to slip the fork under a plant and gently prise it out of position.

Apart from doing all you can to ensure that the soil retains moisture, you also have to water beans well in dry weather, otherwise there is a tendency for the blossom to drop. Once the pods are formed you can feed the plants with liquid manure should you think that the soil is not rich enough or that the pods are not swelling quickly or large enough.

Beetroot

Beetroots vary more than most non-gardeners realise. There are those we grow especially for their succulent roots and those whose roots are not worth cooking but which produce an abundant leaf crop. One is called beetroot and the other leaf beet, or since the beet belongs to the same family, spinach beet. However, beetroot leaves can also be eaten as spinach as you would expect and I certainly never waste a leaf on mine. These leaves have a slightly red colouring, although if you pick off the more vivid stems this is hardly noticeable, but because some people object to this there are beetroots whose leaves are as green as those of the leaf beet. Cheltenham Green-top is one of these and the new Burpees Golden Beet another. You can pick the odd leaf from each beet as these are growing. If you have a freezer you can deal with all the Cheltenham Green-top at the time you lift the roots for storing.

Beetroots themselves, like leaf beets, vary. Those people who have bought only the globe type are sometimes surprised to learn that there are also long, parsnip-shaped varieties, and the Cheltenham Green-top already mentioned is the most popular of these. There are also long, cylindrical varieties such as Dobies Housewives' Choice and Unwin's Formanova. The advantages of these are that they have the deep colour of the glove varieties and you can cut them into even sized slices. In some seasons beetroots bolt quickly. Boltardy has been bred to be long standing, and Unwin's Dwergina remains small, so that it keeps its baby-beet size, handy if you wish to can or pickle the roots.

The most revolutionary change in the varieties is in the introduction of golden and white-rooted types. The advantage, if you consider it one, is that their juice does not stain other foods as the juice of the deep red roots does, but personally I do not think the flavour is as good, although when pulled young the roots are quite delicious.

I do not any longer grow the long beet, simply because I think that the globe beets are better, apart from the fact that they do not occupy the ground for such a long time, are more useful as a summer salad and one can raise them in succession. If I have too many of these at one time I freeze them, although I have also stored them quite well. However, the long-rooted varieties can be stored for a longer period, and of course you can always grow both kinds to gain the virtues of both. One small point, the round roots are much easier to fit into an average sized saucepan. You should not cut the long roots or they will 'bleed' and lose their colour. Often when I have a row of really young roots at the end of summer I cover them with cloches and so am able to continue pulling them for some time into the autumn.

You should not sow beetroot on freshly manured ground because this tends to make them forked and misshapen. It is best to follow a crop for which you liberally manured and fed the soil. If you grow only globe varieties you can start to sow the seed outdoors in April. It is not much good doing this earlier unless you are in a very favoured spot, because the soil will not be warm enough, although as I have suggested elsewhere you can warm it up by using cloches.

The first sowing will provide early summer salads. Reckon on 16 weeks for them to grow to a good size. By using my close-together method I begin to pull really baby beets in June, pulling the largest I can see although only an inch or so in diameter and leaving those near them to swell. By continuing to do this every few days I can extend the season quite considerably. The long beet, which you usually do not lift until you are ready to store them, should be sown from mid-May to early June. You can then lift them from October to November.

Beetroot 'seeds' are large enough to sow separately. Actually each 'seed' is a capsule containing several. I think that it is best to pour the seeds into a dish so that you can handle them easily one by one. Make 1½–2ins deep drills. I do not use the much recommended method of sowing two or three seeds at 4ins spaces. Instead, I space them along the shallow drill so that they are about 2ins apart. If I find that all the seeds in the capsule have germinated, giving a little cluster of plants, I let these grow to a few inches high and then pull them to cook, leaving the largest and spacing the plants out as I do so.

If you have cloches or frames then you can make an earlier start. You can sow from the beginning of March, keeping them under cloches until the frosts are over. Continue sowing each month until July. If you make a hot bed you can force baby beets. Sow in February and March. Give the plants plenty of ventilation.

Beetroots prefer a sandy soil, but not many of us can provide this although we can ensure that the soil is light and open with plenty of humus and peat. Here though we must take care, because the crop does not do well in an acid soil. It is important to dress the soil well with lime before drawing the drill, and to make sure that the soil is rich enough. Use some well balanced fertiliser.

Leaf Beet. If you grow some leaf beet you need never be without good, green vegetables. Treat it just as you would the true spinach. For the cook leaf beet is just as versatile and actually a little less trouble because the leaves are so much easier to wash and they do not get so soiled.

Spinach beet is also known as Perpetual Spinach, possibly because its season is so much longer. You can sow the seed in spring for summer use and in the autumn for winter and spring. Often enough the spring sown plants will go on and on, through summer, autumn and winter until the following spring. I find that I dig mine out at the time the new crop is sown.

There are two very handsome varieties of leaf beet. One of these is the Silver or Seakale Beet, known also as Swiss Chard. The chards are the thick white midribs and stems. These are usually cooked separately and in the same way as seakale, the green being stripped to cook as spinach.

From the Swiss Chard has come the gorgeous Ruby Chard, with vivid magenta stems and dark ruby leaves. It can be cooked in just the same way. It makes a good deep coloured soup not unlike borsch. It also makes a very handsome garden plant.

Grow leaf beets in exactly the same conditions as beetroots.

When you gather leaf beets, go along the row taking the outer leaves, one or two from each plant, according to your requirements. As I have explained elsewhere, I think it is a good plan to cut them back in early autumn before the frosts become severe. The plants seem to become rejuvenated and produce a crop of good young leaves within two months. I find it worth while to cover the cut row with cloches, because then I always have the leaves, otherwise should they become frosted I have to wait until the frost has thawed out of the tissues and the leaves are sound again. I have found also that frosts make the chards very fibrous.

Broccoli

Many people are bewildered when they try to sort out the many varieties of broccoli which they see displayed on a seed packet stand, and sometimes even when they go shopping for kinds to cook. For this reason I think that it might be useful if I left gardening for a moment and took up botany to explain that one of the genus Brassica, a member of Cruciferae, the wallflower family, has been a splendid friend to mankind and to the northern peoples in particular. This is *Brassica oleracea*. Under cultivation it became, and still becomes, so variable that it has produced plants very different in appearance from the species. These include kales, savoy, palm cabbage, red and white cabbage, kohl-rabi, Brussels sprouts, sprouting broccoli and cauliflowers, all related to each other, all developing from one useful source. Generally speaking, horticulturally, what suits one suits the other and we group them all, with cousins like turnips, swedes, Chinese mustard and others under the collective name of brassicas. These, as you will know, usually form a large proportion of our normal garden produce. These vegetables have been developed from the many varieties of *B. oleracea* and bred so that the particular tendency of the plant has been exploited. Thus broccoli has been produced from *B. oleracea cymosa*, which is, to quote the R.H.S. Dictionary of Gardening, 'corymbose with minute flower buds at the tip of fleshy branches'; while cauliflowers have been produced from *B.o. cauliflora*, whose inflorescence is 'very dense often more or less covered by the incurving leaves'.

Many people, especially greengrocers, call certain cauliflowers broccoli when I would call them winter cauliflowers, and I would use the Italian name only for the sprouting and not the tight-headed kinds. I have been told that this misnomer has come about because these vegetables were originally imported out of season from Italy, where all the flower-sprouting brassicas, purple, green or white, tight or bunched, are known as broccoli, and that this was how the fallacy that cauliflowers which appeared in the spring were really broccoli (in the English sense) became established. So, to make sure that we understand each other, I emphasise that in this section I am referring only to those vegetables which have been derived from *B.o. cymosa*.

Incidentally, it is worth recording that broccoli has the highest vitamin content of any vegetable.

But before discussing the varieties of broccoli I should explain about seed sowing, and it should be noted that these remarks apply to all brassicas and not only to broccoli.

It is traditional and very often convenient to prepare a little seed bed or nursery bed in which the seed can be sown in good soil in short rows. Ideally, the bed should also be large enough to take the plants when they are ready to be transplanted, which in spite of the giant brassica plants you may have seen on sale, ought really to be as soon as they are large enough to handle. They should not be left to grow thickly. If they do they will become leggy or drawn in both top and root. The long taproot which crowded plants produce becomes snapped off when you lift them, and although on transplantation a long brassica root does eventually grow more fibrous roots, this takes time. Meanwhile the leafy part of the plant suffers. Plants treated this way seldom crop well, or if they do they take very much longer about it.

In a nursery bed the transplanted seedlings need be only 3ins apart each way. The move stimulates the plants to make a mass of fibrous roots, and when the plants later are moved they do not suffer a great check. They get away quickly, which is what one wants.

However, here as elsewhere and with other subjects, you may find that you have to compromise. What happens, for instance, if you really cannot find enough space to make a nursery bed? In that case simply sow the seeds thinly in a row across the garden and transplant from there. And as so many types of brassica need to be sown at about the same time, you might be able to divide the row so that it takes more than one kind. Here again though, do not let the plants remain crowded.

If you have a small garden you may find that even a small packet of seed may give you more than you need. Not all seed keeps well enough to use another year. It might be economic and certainly more interesting, if you arrange to share with a friend seeds or seedlings of those kinds of vegetables which can be transplanted.

So far as the merits of green or white (white is green as in grapes) or purple sprouting broccoli is concerned, the deciding factor should be the climate of your garden. The white kinds cannot withstand frost as well as the purple. I think that there is not a great deal of difference in the flavour, but of course taste is such a personal thing, and there are those who believe the white to be superior enough to warrant going to some trouble to grow it. Naturally, northern gardeners should expect the crops to mature a little later than they do in the south.

You can expect to gather, in average years: Early Purple Sprouting in January or February and for it to go on for some weeks (and this applies to all varieties); Purple Sprouting in March; Late Purple Sprouting in April; Early White Sprouting in February and Late White in April. All of these behave in very much the same way, beginning by sending up a few large shoots on each plant. Snap these off or cut them off down to a leaf. As one lot is gathered, more but smaller shoots are produced, and after these are picked smaller ones still appear, and it is at this point that you have to decide whether or not to pull up the plants.

After these there is a broccoli gap until August, during which month the delicious summer broccoli, the jade-green, succulent Calabrese develops. This is slightly different in habit from the other sprouting broccoli in that it first produces a large central head. When this is cut shoots are produced from the axils of the leaves round about it. These are never as large as the central head. Cut them quite long, 6ins or more, and indeed, the very latest and smallest shoots can sometimes be cut as long as a foot, with the stem still soft and succulent rather than fibrous. The plants will go on producing shoots for two or three months.

The best of the first, in my opinion, is Suttons Express Corona which is an F1 hybrid. It produces a magnificent first head and masses of shoots afterwards. Another calabrese called Italian Sprouting, matures in September, and yet another, Autumn Spear, is productive from September to November. When you consider that the hardy purple sprouting variety in mild winters will begin shooting in December, you can see what a long season can be planned.

I must point out, however, that sprouting broccoli produces large plants and you need to give them at least $2\frac{1}{2}$ft each way. If you plant them too close you will find that they will not stay in line but will push out one way or another to find themselves growing space.

For autumn-cropping kinds sow seeds in February, and in this case sow them in boxes of light soil and keep them in a temperature of about 17°C (65°F). Transplant them 3ins each way still in a protected place, i.e., in a cold frame or under a cloche, in April or May. In June plant them in their final stations, 2–$2\frac{1}{2}$ft apart. Sow all of the others in April or May and plant them out in or by June or July.

Soil for broccoli does not need to be greatly enriched. Indeed, if it is too rich the plants will grow so lush that they will succumb to frost. It is important, as it is with most brassicas, to plant them firmly. Go along the row after planting and by carefully putting a foot on each side of the stem make sure that each plant is well and truly firmed into position.

Brussels sprouts

Unlike broccoli, Brussels sprouts need good, rich soil and it should be reasonably heavy. Sprouts do not grow well on light soil, mainly because this cannot be sufficiently firmed around their roots and this firming is quite important. Plants which have not been well firmed seldom produce good tight sprouts.

This crop will grow almost anywhere, but as you would expect, the less exposed the site the better. Apart from anything else, it is not pleasant standing picking sprouts in a bitter east wind. Plant in well manured soil which has also been well limed (though not at the same time) and keep it well mulched during the summer. Use a balanced artificial fertiliser as a boost from time to time.

So far as sowing time is concerned much depends on when you wish to gather the sprouts. If you consider them to be purely a winter vegetable you should sow them outdoors in the same way as for broccoli and other brassicas, any time from mid-March to mid-April. They should be ready for planting out 2ft apart each way in May or June. If you grow those varieties which produce very large sprouts, allow 2½ft between the rows.

If you want them earlier than this, select varieties which mature early, such as Roodnerf Early Button, British All Rounder and Early Half Tall. You can sow these in boxes in a cold frame or under cloches at any time from the beginning of January until early February. Some gardeners sow seed outdoors in August to raise plants to harvest in autumn the following year, but actually with modern quick maturing varieties this could be a waste of time and space.

Those who have small gardens can find Brussels sprouts to suit their needs, for there are neat, long-standing types such as Peer Gynt, which is usually ready for first cropping in October, or Early Dwarf and others. And for those who find that it is in the early part of the year that green vegetables are most useful, there are late varieties such as Fasolt Novelty, which remains fit and firm until about mid-February, Roodnerf-Vremo Inter and others. It pays to study a seed catalogue so that you can find the variety best suited to your requirements.

On the other hand, if you have a winter-cold garden and a deep freeze, you might be advised to grow an early variety and pick and freeze ready for winter.

Occasionally someone asks me if it is correct that the tops of sprouts should be removed in order to stimulate sluggish sprouts into growth. There is something in topping, but not to such an extent as to behead the plant while it still produces sprouts. The facts are these.

In order to get early sprouts at the end of August or the beginning of September, some gardeners take out the very heart of the top, removing a piece not much larger than a thumb nail. This has to be done with care, because if too much is taken out or if the plants are not well grown enough, instead of plenty of neat, tight sprouts, the plant will produce blowsy, open ones instead. Also, and especially in a slow season, this operation is carried out in the early winter to help stimulate the growth of those tiny sprouts, usually at the top of the stem, which seem to be hanging fire. Later in the season, when the plants are larger than they are in the summer, the piece nipped out from the heart can be larger also, say as large as a sprout itself. However, I must confess that I do none of this; I prefer to take the sprouts as they come.

Towards the end of the season often the very top sprouts do not swell very much and as the days grow longer they tend to elongate. It is at this period that all of the top of the plant can be cut off and the whole cooked as spring greens. Obviously, if you have managed to pick all the sprouts the same applies. Harvest the tops and pull up and compost the stumps.

When you gather them strip the leaves from the stem base up to the point where the sprouts are large enough. Take a few from each plant in turn, for this way you will extend the season. You should be able to snap them off the stem by pressing them downwards. If you find any 'blown' sprouts remove these also, so that the lower part of the stem is gradually completely cleared. If you are short of greens you can pick and cook the young leaves instead of composting them.

I like to transplant the seedlings when they are really small and I have found this a good move in long, dry summers when the plants seem to grow much better than many around them.

Cabbage

It is possible to cut cabbages the year round but not all of us want them every week of the year. If you prefer to fill your summer garden with a variety of vegetables other than cabbage, you can easily concentrate on those varieties which can be cut in autumn, winter or spring.

However, if you want summer cabbage, then you should begin sowing seed in the early part of the year, during January or the beginning of February in boxes in cold frames or under cloches. Plant them out in late March or early April. If you have enough cloches and the space to spare you can also sow a row or rows very thinly across the garden. Thin the seedlings later to $1\frac{1}{2}$ to 2ft apart, according to the size of the variety, and let them mature *in situ*. You can transplant the thinnings if you wish, but naturally these will mature later. The seeds under cloches should give you cabbages to cut at the end of May or the beginning of June. For this purpose sow only those varieties which are bred and recommended for spring sowing because these mature more quickly. Many of them are also compact and long-standing, ideal for small gardens. Some of them can be staggered, Golden Acre, May Express and Earliest, for example, which can be used for the early-in-the-year sowing under glass, when it should be ready to cut at the end of May or the beginning of June, and then you can make another sowing outdoors from March to June for little, quick maturing cabbages. For July crops sow early in March and plant out in April. Sow in early April for August and at the end of April for September. A pinch from the same packet of seed should see you through.

A word about spacing. Traditionally 2ft apart each way is recommended, but nowadays there is such a good selection of small, compact varieties for all seasons that you may find this is too much space to allow them. I usually space them 18ins apart because I grow only the small varieties. If I were growing, say, January King, which is a very hardy drumhead variety which matures in December and goes on until the spring, I would plant it 2ft each way.

Not all of the cabbages sown in spring hurry along for summer production. Some of them make autumn and winter crops. The tightly packed Winter Salad is one of these, and although the seed catalogue says that the heads can be cut in November and December, I find myself that I can cut them from October until May, which I think is pretty good value. Seed for these should be sown in April. I like to prick out one row as soon as I can handle the plants, for this gives me the really early heads which make such delicious salads, and I plant out the others as space becomes available.

If you do not plan a long succession of cabbages but aim to have just a few in season, these are the sowing times. Sow outdoors from the end of March to the end of April for late summer and autumn. For winter cabbage sow during May or early June and transplant them as soon as they can be handled, either in nursery beds or in their permanent stations. You can make use of the spaces between the plants to grow a quick catch crop.

Red cabbage. You can treat red cabbage like any of the others. However, remember that it needs a longer maturing period than the green kinds, so for late summer use sow the seed in the open in March, transplanting as soon as you can and watering the plants well if the season is dry.

If like me you enjoy this cabbage as a hot winter vegetable or as a winter salad, you can sow a little later and then protect the crops with cloches. If they are touched with frost they will become damaged. If you want really large heads for pickling, sow the seed in August and winter the seedlings in a cold frame or under a cloche. You can then plant them out at the time you are usually sowing the seed, in March or April.

Cabbages grow best on good soil and it should be richer for those you want to mature quickly. On the other hand, cabbages will grow in almost any kind of soil, although it is said that savoys will do better on poor soil. I deal with these later. Hearts are more solid when the plants are well firmed into the soil.

If you find that your garden becomes very dry in the summer months, and that consequently planting out brings problems, consider sowing the cabbage in the rows where they are to stand for winter and then thin them out as early as you can. If you do this, do not sow the cabbage seed too early, delay it until May. If you want more than one row and if you grow more than one variety, stagger the seed sowing and sow the latest to mature last, even at the end of the month.

I always earth up some soil around the roots and lower stems to steady winter cabbage, and there have even been windy seasons when I have staked them, pushing a cane down close to the stem.

Some pests can be a nuisance in some areas and in some seasons. I deal with these in a section at the end of this book.

Chinese cabbage. This is in a class of its own, in appearance, use, and method of growing. It is a brassica and is known as Pe-Tsai, of which there are varieties such as Mi-Chihili, Wongbok and a new F1 hybrid Wonder Cross. In appearance the plant looks like a cross between a cos lettuce and Swiss chard.

The soil for this crop should be light and should contain plenty of humus. If the leaves are to be succulent the plants must grow fast. The plants will not thrive if they are transplanted, so sow the seed very thinly and thin out the seedlings to 9ins apart. As the seed has to be sown in July, it follows that there may be a dry period. Soak the drill before sowing the seed and keep the seedlings well watered in their early stages.

Savoy cabbage. These have a slightly different flavour and texture from normal cabbage, but they are hardier than cabbage and, as I said earlier, they will grow well on poor soil although they will also flourish on rich. Actually in rich soils they can sometimes grow so large as to present a problem – does one eat savoy for a week? The white heart is deliciously nutty and most suitable for use raw in salads, which gives many people another reason for growing them. Treat them as spring sown cabbages.

Carrots

It took me many years before our soil was clean enough and of the right texture to grow carrots well. After so many failures it now gives me great pleasure to see the rows of ferny leaves stretching across the plot and to be able to lift roots which are not deformed or black with invasions of carrot fly and slugs which once inhabited the heavy, sticky soil.

Fortunately the soil is not stony, for on such soil carrots do not grow well. They grow best and are produced commercially on sandy loam where there is also a high water table. Even though I am not on such soil, because I have gradually been able to lighten it by adding humus it is now able to grow good carrot crops, and this is the case in many other gardens. Furthermore, carrots need moisture, especially in dry summers, and the humus in the soil helps to retain it. I choose varieties which I know will do well and grow only the intermediate or stump-rooted kinds. To ensure that the soil is always porous enough, when I sow the seeds I line the drill with peat as I have explained earlier.

The lighter and more open the soil the more quickly will the roots swell, and it should be so textured that you can easily pull young carrots. If you have to tug at them or even fork them up something is wrong, which you will soon see once you have the roots in your hand. Instead of being plump and succulent they will be thin and tough. On the other hand, I should say that in dry weather even good roots will not always come out easily. At such a time it helps if you water the row the evening before you intend to pull them.

It is best to sow carrots on land which has been previously manured for another crop. If the soil has been freshly manured the roots will tend to fork and be very fibrous. You also have to take care about which artificial fertilisers you use. For instance, too much nitrogen causes them to split their roots. I find that they do very well when I spread plenty of well-rotted compost on the strip of land where they are to be sown. Just before sowing I like to dress the soil with a balanced fertiliser. Carrots should be able to get away to a good start.

If you use my peat-lined drill method, there are a few points you should observe. First see that the drill is well soaked before you sow the seed. Carrots will not germinate well if the seed suffers from drought. See also that you put in sufficient peat to raise the level, so that when the seed is sown it need be covered by only the shallowest covering of soil, ¾ to ½in or so, just enough to weight it down. Firm the soil after sowing and water it again after covering the seed, using a fine rose so that you do not disturb the soil and wash the seed out.

If you have to make a decision about what is economical to grow and what is not, I suggest that you concentrate on young carrots and buy those big roots you need in winter. The first are always quite expensive, and although tasty enough they are never as good as those you pull fresh and eat right away. These young carrots, bunched carrots to the trade, can be produced quite early in a warmed frame, a hot bed, in cold frames and under cloches. The last is obviously best for the beginner gardener. According to the clemency of the season, sow them in January or February, obviously the earlier the better. If you have to share out the space under your cloches, consider growing lettuces with the carrots. You can sow them between the rows of lettuces and they will grow up above them. You can also broadcast the seed over the cloche-wide row (but you will need to leave a margin on each side to keep the plants from pressing against the cloche glass) and mix it with radish. The last will mature earlier and can be pulled and out of the way before the carrots are ready for cropping. If you have peas, beans or leaf beet under cloches, the carrots can be sown alongside. The shallow drill you draw for their seed is not likely to disturb the roots of the other crops.

If you have a sheltered bed somewhere, perhaps at the foot of a wall or fence, and so long as the soil is light or has been made light, you can sow a really quick maturing variety such as Champion Scarlet Horn or the very early Amstel, in the open in early March. You can also sow any one of these or other quick maturers in March and April in the open garden. Naturally they will do better under cloches, and as I have suggested else-where, if you have only two or three cloches to spare it is sometimes worth covering only part of a row.

These early sown crops should give you roots which you can begin pulling, as thinnings at first, in June and on through to July. Reckon three months for intermediate types to mature. Any of the early varieties can be sown in succession up to the middle of July. It is a good scheme to sow the next batch as soon as you see the previous one appearing above the soil. If you learn to sow very thinly you can make a packet of seed go a long way. I don't sow radish with carrot because this would mean that the soil would become disturbed too often, and apparently loose soil offers the carrot root fly an easy way in. It is advisable always to firm the soil after you have pulled any roots, even the small thinnings.

If you would like to pull young carrots in November and December, sow an *early* variety in September or October, or even in August if you live in a cold district. Cover them with cloches in October.

If you would like to store carrots for winter use, sow them in May or early June, or if space is at a premium, early in July, when you may be able to follow a lettuce or some other green crop. You need to grow them well enough for them to make good roots by October or the beginning of November. The July sown roots should be large enough by this time. Of course you can pull some of these as young carrots if you have no others and you can use the thinnings. By the end of the year the carrots begin to slow down their rate of growth. You can leave them in the soil and lift them as you need them. I have sometimes done this quite satisfactorily and it seems to work well except when the soil is frosted, and of course roots left in the soil can be eaten by slugs or mice. One winter the carrots were completely scooped out by mice. When I went to pull them I found just the crown left. This, surprisingly, had managed to sustain the leafy tops, so that by looking at the plants there was no indication of the tragedy below soil level. For these reasons it is often much more convenient to lift and store the roots in boxes or bins of dry earth, sand or peat, which should be kept in a frostproof shed or cellar.

When you lift them choose a dry day. Use a fork thrust in deep along the row to loosen the roots and to prise them up a little, and then pull them out by hand, shaking off any loose soil. Sort them over, remove any which are not first class, damaged, or cracked, and set these aside for immediate use or for freezing. Cut off the leaves as near to the crown of the plant as possible without damaging it. This is to prevent more leaves growing during storage. Lay the roots somewhere where they can dry in the air before you store them, but make sure that you do not let them dry too much or they will become shrivelled. A few hours is usually sufficient. Turn them once or twice.

To store, first place a layer of the store material, soil or whatever, in the box about 2ins deep. Arrange a layer of roots on this. You can get more in if you pack them like sardines, top to tail in rows. Cover with another layer of soil, make another root layer and continue this way until the box is almost full. Finish with a topping of soil.

When wooden boxes are used I think it is best to raise them a little from the floor so that air can pass beneath them. Stand them on four bricks or wooden slats.

Cauliflowers

This is a crop which can bring you either a splendid feeling of triumph or one of great disappointment. So much depends upon your soil, the season and the variety you choose to grow as well as what time of year you grow it. Generally speaking these are not plants for the very small garden. Most of the varieties make large plants and once you have cut the head, although you can cook the youngest leaves as greens, there are no side shoots to follow as there are in other heading brassicas.

You should also take into consideration that a row of cauliflowers tends to mature all at the same time, although I suggest that if this is not convenient to you, you begin cutting some before they are really ready. Once upon a time the crop had largely to be given away or used up quickly – hence so much cauliflower pickle. Nowadays those with a deep freeze are more likely to find a row maturing about the same time and welcome it as both convenient and profitable.

Seed catalogues contain lists of so many varieties that I feel sure that many beginner gardeners must be confused and wonder which one they should choose for their own gardens. I suggest that if you have never grown cauliflowers before, or perhaps if you have never grown them successfully, that you try one or two well tested varieties which can be grown with the minimum of fuss, such as All the Year Round, or if you want a whopper, Veitch's Autumn Giant or Flora Blanca Algromajo No. 2, which is much the same as the latter. These are varieties for spring sowing. I recommend the new Australian varieties if you have a small plot. These are dwarf growing and so take up much less room than some of the more traditional types. If these are sown outdoors in late April or May they will be ready to harvest in September, October or November according to the variety.

Sow the seed in a nursery bed in late April or May. Plant out the seedlings as soon as you can about 18ins apart and 2ft between the rows. From this point on never let them suffer from drought. The soil must be adequately limed or the plants will not flourish. This applies also to the nursery bed. However, take care that you do not overdo this. It must also be rich and retentive of moisture. On the other hand, do not try to grow the plants in newly manured soil or they will grow too rank and will not produce tight curds.

If you have a sheltered garden you can grow some of the so-called winter cauliflowers. These should produce heads from January to May according to the variety. There are some extra hardy types such as some of the English Winter varieties, some of which have proved to grow best in the north of the country. These also are sown in late April and May.

Varieties differ in their habit of growth. 'Self-protecting' means that the leaves grow over, and so protect, the curds. If you grow a non-self-protecting variety, when the curd begins to form and is growing well, you should snap the midrib of some of the outer leaves so that they fold over and make a roof for the curds. Unprotected curds can become discoloured by the weather and so are perhaps less pleasing to the eye than pure, creamy white, but on the other hand they lose nothing in their flavour or their vitamin content.

Celeriac

This is a much easier crop than one might imagine and the swollen roots are so useful during winter for salads, as a hot vegetable or for flavourings. I also use the leaves and the thongy side roots for flavouring stock, so you see it really is a good value vegetable. Perhaps I should point out that plants of this vegetable and of celery can be bought from a nurseryman. If you should like to raise your own, remember that the secret of success is to sow the seeds early, in March, indoors in heat, 18–25°C (65–75°F). I use the plastic bag method for these. As soon as they are large enough to handle, prick out the seedlings into boxes 2ins apart each way and keep them growing. They should be maintained at about the same temperature and it might be necessary to keep them in their plastic bags. (See chapter 4, page 41.)

Begin hardening them off in April. They can go into a cold frame at this time. If you fear that they are becoming crowded you can plant them 6ins apart in a nursery bed so long as you can keep the frost from them. Plant them outdoors in June 12ins apart. Choose a sunny site. The soil should be light and rich, with plenty of compost and it helps to mulch it with more during the summer. From time to time give liquid manure to the plants. Be sure to keep them well watered in dry weather, and if you have reason to believe that the soil may become very dry (as in a prolonged spell of sunny weather) it might be wise to draw a drill along the row into which water can be poured from time to time.

In order to get a good sized 'bulb' you should remove all the side shoots which form around the main root mass. You will have to search for these, and to do this gently scrape away the soil from around the plant taking care not to expose the smaller fibrous roots to the air. You should find that the bulb swells and sits more or less above the soil level.

By the end of August, although it may be later, when the bulbs are well grown, begin gradually to earth up some soil around the roots so that they will receive some protection by the time the frosts arrive.

The roots should be large enough to lift and store in October or November. Of course you can dig some to use before this date if you like. Let them dry, twist off the leaves, retaining the little centre shoot intact, and store them in the same way as advised for carrots. With a sharp knife cut away the thongy roots trimming them flush with the bulb. Alternatively, you can leave them in the soil, but if you do so be sure that the roots are well protected with soil drawn up around them like a coverlet.

Celery

If you feel that you would like to try your hand at celery, may I suggest that you begin with one or other of the summer types. If you grow these successfully you can move on to the winter kinds. Cultivation of these is much more arduous and includes the making of trenches, although even here I think that one can compromise. Nevertheless, I do not think that winter celery is a beginner's crop.

There are now two kinds of summer celery, white and green. The latter is an American type and although green is not, as one might imagine, stringy and indigestible.

The advantage of these types is that they do not need earthing up. The disadvantage is that they succumb to frosts and are not very long-standing. Once they are ready they have to be eaten.

These varieties are not planted in rows but in blocks, by which means they protect and blanch each other. They can be grown in a frame and this is generally considered to be the best and easiest method. You can get 2 doz or so in a 6 by 4ft frame, planted 9ins apart, or you can surround the plants with boards or black plastic sheeting.

Raise the seed in the same way as suggested for celeriac, but sow it in mid-March, a week or two later. The seed is sometimes slow to germinate.

Whether in a frame or outside, the soil for celery should be made rich, and if you incorporate plenty of well rotted compost, peat, or any rich soil mixture you can buy such as spent mushroom compost, you will also make it moisture retentive. If you find it difficult to get any of these and the humus content is high, use a good balanced fertiliser. Lime the bed well before you plant it.

When you place out the little celery plants you can interspace them with lettuce which has been raised indoors from seed sown a month before the celery. You should then find that it is mature before the celery crowds it.

Use plenty of slug pellets all the time this crop is under cultivation. From July onwards you need to water the plants liberally. This alone will tend to attract slugs, although they find the plants to their liking also. During this time you should also feed the plants frequently with a weak liquid manure.

In spite of its name, Self-blanching celery still needs to have as much light kept from the stems as possible. As you will appreciate, the plants in the centre of a block will be more protected than those on the outside. If light gets to them they will become greener. When you dig the outer plants, move the boards or whatever you use close to the next row. A piece of board, even a light hardboard will do, is easily kept in place by pushing a few canes close up to it.

The American Green varieties of celery are said not to require earthing up or blanching.

Chicory
This crop calls for patience rather than skill. It is worth having and it is quite easy to grow. Apart from the convenience of having such a delicious salad in mid-winter, the price of chicory in the shops in recent years has rocketed. You may find that at first you don't produce the good looking tight hearts such as you see on sale, but I think that even so you would still find the exercise worth while and you can go on to better things. This seems to be a crop where those who have grown it tend to develop their own pet methods of culture. Some people, for instance, like to let the roots dry on a shelf in a frost-free shed before planting them. I give two methods. You can vary them to suit your own circumstances if need be.

The important thing is to encourage chicory (which is really a perennial in spite of its late sowing) to grow so well in its first season that it develops large roots. These are then lifted, rested for a brief period and then re-planted and forced into growth again. It is these new growths that are the chicons. Allowed to grow naturally they are very green and inedible. Even the tiny thinnings one pulls from a seed row are bitter. Grown in darkness the leaves become elongated and blanched. They are then sweet and digestible. Chicory is sown late to prevent it flowering, late May or early June is the time. Sow thinly in very shallow drills, and if you grow more than one row, set them 1ft apart. Thin the plants to 9ins apart.

Other than keeping the plants weeded, no other cultural attention is needed until late autumn. They should form large, bright green heads by the end of summer. After this time they will begin to die down so that by the beginning of November they should be ready to be lifted. If you are in a mild area where frosts at this time are unlikely, you can leave the plants in the soil and lift them as you need them. If you think that this is risky, there are two alternatives. You can lift them and heel them in somewhere in a sheltered corner, rather as you lift and heel in flowering bulbs before they have died down. In this case you should heap plenty of soil over the plants so that they really are protected from any frost.

Alternatively, and this method seems to suit most people best, you should lift and trim them and then store them in sand outdoors or in a cool shed or cellar which is frostproof and unlikely to become warm.

The best roots are tapered and should be about 2ins across the top. They should be from 10 to 7ins long and you can cut them at the bases. Trim the leaves, cutting them to within an inch of their bases. At the same time rub off any side shoots if you see them.

There are two methods of planting. The first is as follows. You can use all kinds of containers for forcing. Flower pots can be used in pairs, planting in one and placing the other on top, rim to rim to exclude light. Alternatively, large boxes will do. Stand the roots upright in the containers with the crowns an inch above the soil and 3–5ins apart. You can use ordinary soil. It helps to keep the chicons cleaner if you can top this with a deep layer of clean horticultural sand but this is not essential.

Water the soil and let it drain. Cover the pot or box with another of the same size and close any aperture through which light might penetrate. You can also use black plastic bags drawn over the top of the pots or boxes, but you might have to provide supports for these so that they do not flop over the plants. Alternatively, stand the containers inside the bags.

The filled and covered pots should then be stood in a warm place where the temperature does not fall below 8°C (45°F) and where it rises to 16°C (60°F). The cooler the environment the longer the chicons will take to appear. You can put a pot under the kitchen sink if you have no other place. Certainly they can be grown under the greenhouse staging.

You can begin forcing the roots in December and continue ideally until March, but some people keep them going until early May. Keep the routine going at weekly intervals.

The second is an even easier method which many readers are sure to find much more convenient, especially where it is found difficult either to buy or to store large pots and boxes. Take a black plastic bag of any convenient and suitable size and place in it about 3ins of moist peat. Drop this on the ground once or twice to make a flat base so that it will stand well. In this peat plant the roots you intend to force, wedging and holding them in place with more moist peat. Take this up to their crowns. Then close the bag securely after blowing in it to hold the top and sides off the crowns. Stand the bag in the warm place of your choice and open it for inspection after two or three weeks.

Corn salad

If you like salads, once you have grown corn salad in winter and early spring I think that you are certain to grow it every year. It is one of the important bases of salads on the continent, possibly because it is so hardy. It is one of our native plants, and as its name suggests was once to be found among the corn.

It can be grown the year round, but I think that most gardeners will agree that economically it is at its greatest value during the short days rather than in summer, when there is greater variety available. With corn salad, land cress, endive and lettuce, cabbage, sprouting crops and green herbs, the salad enthusiast can make fine mixed salads all winter through. In summer the crop matures in eight weeks and it will grow almost as fast in winter if it is protected by cloches, otherwise it will take a little longer. If you have only two or three cloches to spare it is worth while covering a few plants. I prefer to cover this crop simply because the leaves grow larger and are more tender than those from plants in the open. It will stand frost and snow in the open.

For winter use sow during August and September and I suggest that you will find it more helpful to make successional sowings at fortnightly intervals. There is, of course, no need to cover them with cloches until October, by which time some should be almost ready to pick.

When the little seedlings have formed three leaves, thin the plants to 6ins apart. You can use the thinnings if you don't mind the fiddly task of washing such tiny plants. They are worth doing if you are short of salad, or you can throw them in with the spinach and cook them.

Gather the crop in the same way that you gather spinach, leaf by leaf in the early stages. You can begin taking one leaf from each plant when they have made four leaves. But never strip a young plant, always allow about half the leaves to remain. Later on I suggest that you begin pulling the entire plant, taking alternate plants, but this must depend on how many plants you have and how long you want them to go on. The plants flower in April, so there is not much point in leaving them in that long, because the flowering stems become tough. When they grow leggy you can use the stems and leaves as, or mixed with, spinach or leaf beet.

Cresses

American or Land cress. If you have a moist, partially shaded border you can cultivate plenty of tasty cress all the year round. I am not sure how this native plant came to be called American, but the fact that it is native and a perennial indicates instantly that it is hardy. All the same, you will find that if you can give it some protection in frosty weather, and you need cover only a few plants at a time, you will have a good supply always on hand.

It much resembles watercress in appearance and taste and it shares a liking for moisture, although it does not, like the former, need to paddle. It will grow in ordinary soil, but this should be rich and contain plenty of humus to retain the moisture.

If you would like to harvest some all the year round, sow the seed from March to June for summer eating and in September for winter. Reckon from 10 to 12 weeks for it to be ready to cut. Summer crops should be liberally watered or the leaves will be tough and not a good flavour. Sow the seed thinly either in drills or broadcast and thin them to about 4ins apart. I suggest that you let the seedlings grow to a useful size and begin harvesting the crop by using the thinnings. Although the plant is a perennial, you will get better crops if you sow fresh seed each year.

Pick it leaf by leaf, taking several leaves from one plant. Do not let it flower. Keep any stems nipped out so that the plants keep their rosette shape.

Cress, Curled with Mustard. This is one of the most useful of the sprouting crops and I suppose that most of us have at one time or another, even if only in childhood, raised enough for a sandwich or two, usually on a piece of wet flannel. This method still works but there are better ones, especially if you want to keep a crop going.

Although you can raise it the year through, I imagine most people will find mustard and cress most useful during winter and early spring when other salads are at a premium.

I have tried various containers and I think that the most convenient are the plastic seed trays which have no drainage hole, particularly if you intend to raise the crop in your home, on a window sill for instance, Although the soil should be moist it should not be watered once the seeds are sown.

Use a light soil. This is best sifted so that it forms a smooth, even surface. It should be moist but not sodden. Test it this way. After moistening it with a fine rose or a sprayer, take a handful and squeeze it tight and then open your hand. The soil particles should cling together and then fall apart immediately when you drop the ball.

Fill the box almost to the rim and then tamp the soil down with a piece of wood or something similar so that it is smooth and level. You can use the same soil twice and then it should be replaced with fresh.

Sow the seed thinly but distribute it evenly in such a way that the surface is covered. You will soon acquire the knack.

From this point you can use two methods. The simplest thing to do is to gently spray the seeds with tepid water from a fine sprayer to soften the hard seed coats, and then cover the box with a sheet of glass, clear plastic or even a sheet of paper and then stand it somewhere in the warm. Ideally, the temperature should be about 18°C (65°F) by day and 10°C (50°F) by night. If it is too warm the seedlings will become very drawn and if too cold they will be stunted.

Uncover the seedlings once they have germinated. Wait until the seed leaves expand and develop fully and then cut them.

The disadvantage of this method sometimes is that the seed cases remain on the seed leaves and they have to be washed carefully to remove them. Not that they would harm you, but they are neither pretty nor palatable. If, however, some way is devised to hold the moisture closer to the seedlings, this does not happen. The practice is to cut pieces of hessian or some similar lightweight, open-weave material, to fit the seed tray. Lay this on the seed and then by using a sprayer keep it constantly moist. The seedlings will push it up. Continue to keep it moist. When the seedlings are about 1 to 1½ins high, remove the cover and allow them to turn green.

Some people grow mustard only and others like to mix mustard with cress. It is important to remember that the two do not take the same length of time to germinate. Cress should be sown three days earlier than mustard for them both to be cropped at the same time. So if you want to grow both crops in the same box, leave space for the mustard seed. Usually a little more mustard than cress is sown in a mixture. As a general rule allow about ¾oz of mustard and ½oz of cress to a seed tray. Buy the seed in quantity. Seedsmen usually sell it by the pound.

If you hope to consume plenty, the next thing is to devise means of obtaining a succession. It takes cress about a week to become tall and green enough to pick, and mustard about four days, although sometimes in winter during the short days the period may be a little longer. It may be best to sow anew every seven days. You will soon learn and can adjust sowing intervals accordingly.

Cucumber

Since this is a book for the beginner gardener I have no intention of going into details for the culture of cucumbers indoors, that is to say, in a greenhouse or a frame. Modern varieties of the less tender and less time demanding outdoor varieties are so good that anyone would be well advised to try them. I grow a different variety each year simply to see what snags they have, and I can truthfully say that all of those I have so far attempted are suitable for beginners. However, it is only fair to add that they do best in hot summers in protected places.

There is only one thing that might deter some people, and that is that the seeds should be raised indoors in heat, but it is possible in most areas to buy ready raised plants of cucumbers. The raising of the seed really is simple and suggestions are made in chapter four.

At the moment of writing my family are enjoying the funny little fat fruits of the Apple Cucumber offered by Suttons, our this year's trial. These plants are growing up tripods made of three canes lashed together and others up the uprights which support the roof mesh of our vegetable cage. I had no idea that the growth would be so abundant nor that there would be so many fruits, but it has been a very hot summer. We find the fruits delicious. They are small, no more than 2–3ins long and 1½–2ins in diameter, so one is just about a serving for one person. We eat them skins and all, slightly prickly but very tender. One or two people to whom I have given some have found the skins bitter and have preferred to peel them.

When I saw the cucumber fruits I realised for the first time why the poisonous wild Mediterranean plant, *Ecballium elaterium*, is called squirting cucumber. The shape of its fruits and those of the apple cucumber are very similar. Until now I had never seen any real sense in the trivial name. For this reason I imagine that this particular cucumber must have been in cultivation for a long time, which may account for its slight bitterness. Modern varieties of cucumber differ from this one in taste as well as appearance. The hybridists have carefully bred out all traces of bitterness from the varieties offered by today's seedsmen. Such apt names as those given by Burpee to some of the varieties are self-explanatory: Burpless Green King, Burpless Tasty Green, Burpless Early. Burpless Tasty Green is much more like the greenhouse varieties which we see in greengrocers' shops than any of the others. It is also resistant to mildew, a disease from which some plants suffer in some seasons. Not only do these cucumbers not cause indigestion (as suggested by the famous and ebullient Mr Burpee), but the plants are very easy to grow. Those who have never before grown cucumbers are, I think, bound to be agreeably surprised by the number of fruits which a plant produces.

It is important to make a good start, so sow the seeds singly, points downwards, in small pots of seed sowing compost indoors in mid-April. I keep mine in their plastic bags until the leaves are really well formed, then I turn down the bag so that the plant is well exposed to the air. After about a week of this I stand the plants out every day, gradually hardening them off. By May they should be well hardened and growing well. They will still have to come indoors at nights in case of frosts. Plant them outdoors during the first week in June.

During this time keep a good watch on the plants to see that they do not become potbound. To check whether or not a pot is full of roots, take the pot in one hand and open the fingers of the other hand, putting them so that the plant is held between two of them. This way the crown of the plant is held fast. Turn the pot upside down and tap its edge sharply against another pot or the edge of a table or shelf. The whole of the root mass, or root ball as it is called, should fall out into the hand rather like a sand pie at the seaside. You should be able to see the roots. If these are more conspicuous than the soil, and especially if some of the roots are pushing their way through the drainage holes at the base of the pots, it is time that the plant was moved on to another, larger pot. Do not think to save time that you will help the plant by giving it a much larger pot than its present home, for this very seldom works. Simply move it into the next size in pots. This will give you only a little extra space under the root ball and a little more all the way round. When the plant is repotted its soil level should be the same as before.

Place a little potting soil in the base of the flower pot. Knock out the plant and stand the root ball on this. Test that the soil level is just below the rim of the pot as it was in the original pot and adjust should this be necessary. Then pour soil down around the space between the root ball and the pot, ramming it in with your fingers as you do so in order to bring the new soil to the same density as the root ball soil. If you do not do this often the roots just will not grow into the new soil, and should you ram the new soil too much the same will happen. After repotting, water the soil thoroughly, let it drain and then wait until it becomes almost dry again before you water again.

When you plant the cucumbers in the garden give them a good site. They do not like cold winds, so try to give them as much protection as you can. Should the weather be cold in the early part of June, protect the plants with cloches so that there is no, or very little, check in their growth.

In the greenhouse cucumbers are given very rich soil indeed, so provide the same to your outdoor plants. Try to make each station warm and cosy (see chapter 4). Prepare each site well. One of the best ways of doing this is to take out a square, 18ins wide and 12ins deep, and fill this with a prepared mixture of 2 parts soil, 1 part well rotted manure or home made compost and 1 part peat. If the season seems cold, first put in a layer of fresh lawn mowings.

You can raise the plants by sowing the seeds where they are to go, in which case you should cover them with cloches. Prepare the site, sow the seeds, water and put down slug pellets. On no account allow the soil to become dry or they will not germinate well or quickly, and when the plants are growing, unless the weather is wet and cold water them well.

When the plants come into bloom give them a balanced fertiliser as a boost.

Keep an eye on the plants all summer. During very hot weather when they are likely to flag quite badly, take a fine rose watering can and soak the leaves and make the soil all around them moist so that there is plenty of humidity generated around them. Do this as a matter of routine in the evenings.

Cucumbers can be affected by something called collar rot, said to be caused by allowing water or liquid manure to splash up against the main stem. I take great care when I water my plants to pour the water on to the soil at some distance, at least 3–4ins, from the main stem so that there is no risk of this happening, and so far none of my plants have suffered this disease.

Indoor cucumbers have to be carefully trained, but I suggest that you ignore this for outdoor varieties. We seldom get the ideal weather conditions where the plants are likely to grow out of control, and it is my experience that if you let them grow quite naturally you will reap a crop large enough to satisfy your wishes.

Dandelion

So far as I am concerned, up till now the dandelions I have eaten in my own home have all been nature's gifts. I simply leave unweeded those plants which appear in or near the vegetable patch, and in early spring I cover each with a large clay flower pot, close the hole with a cork, slip a few slug pellets under it and wait for the leaves to blanch which they do very well. Once I have gathered them I lift the root and burn it – a very useful and productive form of weeding.

These blanched leaves are elongated, but the cultivated forms which have naturally thicker leaves are sometimes more substantial when forced. The leaves also can be eaten green and they are especially good in spring. However, some people find them a little bitter, and when they are green, true to their French name, 'pis-en-lit', they sometimes tend to have a diuretic effect. Even so many people find the dandelion a useful and easy to grow salad, and others lift, wash, dry and roast the roots to make coffee. Roots and leaves may be bought bunched, neat and cherished in market places in France, Germany, Switzerland and certain other northern continental countries. The flowers can be made into an excellent wine. Many of our seedsmen now list a culinary dandelion, larger and possibly improved compared to our uninvited weed, but it seems questionable whether it is worth the extra cost except, perhaps, to the gourmet.

As well as being blanched by covering them in the way I have described, the roots can also be lifted, stored and treated from then on in the same way as chicory. This is a good, clean way of growing them. A more simple way to blanch them is merely to pile peat or soil over them, but if you do this you should watch for and guard against slugs. It is always wise to put down a few pellets near the plants.

They will grow well in almost any soil and situation, but they do best in a sunny site and in ground which has not been recently manured. Sow the seed in 1in deep drills in April. Thin the seedlings to 6ins apart. Keep the flowers picked off as soon as they begin to form. Let them open if you want to make wine with them, but watch that you do not let them go to seed or you will have more weeds than you want, and so, most likely, will your neighbours.

Lift the roots in November. You can plant the roots closer than you would chicory, they can be almost touching. Plant in any good ordinary soil in pots or boxes or use bags of peat as suggested for chicory.

Endive

Endive and chicory belong to the same family, indeed in some countries the names have become interchanged. For instance, Americans mean what we call chicory when they refer to endive. There are basically two types or classes, one which has fairly narrow, fern-like leaves known as curled, and one which is broad leaved, sometimes called Batavian or sometimes lettuce-leaved endive. The latter type is the hardiest, but the former is the more popular and is the tenderest of the two.

Endive is not the easiest of crops because so much depends upon the season and the locality of the garden where it grows, for although we look on this mainly as a winter vegetable, endive will not stand hard frost. Those who live in the warm districts of these islands will probably be able to grow it outdoors in winter, but generally you should be prepared to use cloches. In cool areas the plants should be covered by September or October, according to the season.

You can have endive in summer, and for this purpose you should sow the seed outdoors in very shallow drills from April onwards, but be warned: plants from early summer sowings often run to seed, as do those which are transplanted in summer. It is best to thin out the plants, not transplant them, during the summer months. Endive is not grown much in summer simply because lettuce is so much easier to produce. For late autumn and winter crops you can sow the seed in late June, July and August. The broad-leaved kind should be sown late.

Sow the seed thinly in shallow drills just scratched out of the surface. If the weather is cool wait for higher temperatures. You can thin out or transplant the seedlings to 1ft to 15ins apart. I transplant a row in September on the edge of the raised border along the side of my vegetable garden path. Here the soil is light, rich, well drained and warm. The plants are also protected by the other plants behind them. It is important to water the plants freely in dry weather because they must be encouraged to grow fast and not to run to seed.

Like chicory, endive must be blanched otherwise it is bitter, but in its case the roots are not lifted, instead the growing plant is covered. There are various methods used to blanch the plants and I give here some of the more simple ones.

The process usually takes about 10–14 days. Blanch only two or three at a time and stagger this process because blanched plants do not keep well. One method is that which we once used to blanch the old varieties of cos lettuce, which is simply to tie the leaves so that light is shut out from the heart of the plant. In the case of endive you must first bring the leaves up from the ground. Tie a piece of raffia around the centre of the plant, pulling it as tight as you can without actually damaging the leaves. I suggest that you finish off with a loop so that you can return from time to time and tighten the tie.

You can also use the method I employ for my weed dandelions, and simply invert a flower pot over a plant. Again lift up the outer leaves before you do this and be sure to plug the drainage hole of the pot so that no light shines through.

Yet another method is to put a plate or bowl on each plant. Place it face downwards so that it does not sit tightly on the centre.

If you grow the plants under cloches you can cover a cloche with black plastic sheeting, which is a quick and easy method. You can also pull up a plant and its roots and place it in an absolutely dark location such as a cellar for a few days.

There is also a method which involves lifting the plants and transplanting them to frames, but I suggest that as this calls for certain skill and takes both time and frame space, it really does not have a place in a book for beginners.

Whichever method you use, be quite sure that the plants are dry before you tie them up or cover them.

Florence fennel
This is a variety of *Foeniculum vulgare*, the tall herb grown for flavouring. It is grown as an annual and is valued for its swollen leaf bases which together form a bulbous growth which can be cooked or very finely sliced and eaten raw.

It is one of the most delicious, and from the gardener's point of view also one of the most disappointing vegetables. It must have rich soil and almost unlimited quantities of water, which means that in dry summers the crop is often a failure.

Sow the seeds in succession from April to August. I suggest that you take note of which sowings do best in your garden and in future stick to these.

Thin the seedlings to 9ins apart and keep them growing well, watering them and giving them liquid manure from time to time. When you notice the bases of the stalk beginning to thicken, earth them up rather as you would a potato plant. Usually the plants can be used about a month after this. In fact, to make the crop last I suggest that the best procedure is to begin using the biggest of the young bulbs. The earthing up process also serves to blanch them.

When you gather them, cut the leaves right down to the bulb. If you wish these can be dried for herbs.

Kale

The greatest value of this vegetable lies in its hardiness, which means that it can be relied upon to come through the severest winter and to produce greens in spring and early summer when others may be scarce. It will also flourish in poor soils. Indeed, it should not be finally planted in soil which is very rich in nitrogen because then the plants may become too soft, in which case they will not winter well.

Treat kale like any other brassica. Sow the seeds thinly in April and May. Do not let the seedlings become crowded. Keep them transplanted if they cannot be put into their permanent rows, so that the plants grow stocky and strong.

Curly kales are favourites, but one should be warned that the leaves often need scrupulous washing, especially if the crop is grown near towns. Dirt tends to nestle in the frills of the leaves. If you can get it, Cottagers Kale has plainer, purple-tinged leaves.

Seedsmen do not seem to list as many varieties of kale as once they did, perhaps the demand has dropped, which would be a pity because this is a useful vegetable. If you cook an onion with kale or any other brassica the greens will be sweeter and will not give off a cabbagy smell which is offensive to some people.

Kohl-rabi

Asked to describe kohl-rabi, I think I would say that it is a cross between a cabbage and a turnip. Certainly the colour of the leaves more resembles that lovely jade green of the leafy vegetable, while the swollen leaf stalks grow to the size and shape of a turnip. Its great value lies in its hardiness, for it will tolerate drought and withstand considerable frost. Both the swollen root and the leaves can be cooked. The former should be skinned and sliced and then boiled, stewed or steamed, and the leaves cooked like cabbage.

The plants can be treated like any other brassicas, i.e., sown in a seed bed and transplanted, or they may be sown where they are to mature and then be thinned out.

The seed can be sown in shallow drills in April and May for summer succession, and onwards into June to produce a winter crop.

Plants can be left outdoors all winter and lifted when required. It is important that the roots are not allowed to grow too large. Pull them when they are about the size of a tennis ball.

Sow thinly and thin the seedlings to 3ins apart and then pull alternate plants when the roots are sufficiently swollen. Water the plants well after transplanting and thinning.

Leeks

This is one of the most useful vegetables in the kitchen garden especially in winter, for it is completely hardy and can be dug up as required. It is delicious cooked, as most people know, but I would recommend you also to use it finely sliced in salads.

Leek enthusiasts all seem to have their own pet way of growing this vegetable. I tend to use what I think is the easiest method, which is to sow the plants thinly in the open ground in spring, from early March to mid-April according to season. They can be sown either in a prepared bed, where they can stay until space becomes available for them elsewhere, or they can be sown in a row across the garden.

They should be transplanted when they are about 6ins high and the usual and easy method of planting is as follows. With a garden line as a guide, at 9ins intervals make holes with a dibber some 6ins deep and drop a plant into each hole. Water it in. You will appreciate that good porous soil is most easily dibbled, and although leeks seem to grow well in almost any soil I find that they seem to do best in land which is rich in humus. If your soil is heavy, try filling the dibbled holes with peat after dropping the leek in. Don't bury its leaves. These should project above the soil.

If you do not want the trouble of planting out the leeks and as long as you have the space to spare, you can simply sow the seed very thinly and then later thin the seedlings to 2ins apart. Leave a foot between the rows. Or you can compromise in this way. Sow one or more rows, thin out and transplant the thinnings, leaving the other plants to mature where they were sown.

The portion of root which grows below the soil is blanched, and you can blanch a greater portion of the stem if you also earth up the plants. Do this during late summer and autumn.

A fiddling point perhaps, but one which saves a little space: study the plants and drop them into the holes in such a way that the leaves point along the rows and not at right angles to it.

If by spring you have not used all your leeks and you notice that they are beginning to elongate preparatory to flowering, lift them and heel them in close together in some odd corner. Simply make a narrow trench with spade or fork as deep as the blanched roots. Lay them against one side of it, cover them with earth and thereafter pull them as required. This will slow them down.

Lettuce

At one time the lettuces most of us grew were neatly divided into two types, cabbage and cos, but now there are also intermediate kinds which seem to have a little of each of the other's characteristics in them but which still come under the omnibus cabbage description. These are the Crisp Heart varieties which have full white hearts, of which the best known is probably Webb's Wonderful. The other kind, soft leaved and round with yellow hearts are now grouped under the term Butterhead and their leaves really do seem to be more oily or buttery than the crisphead or cos varieties. There are also the loose leaf or cutting lettuces such as Salad Bowl and Grand Rapids which do not make tight hearts in the same way as the others and which can be gathered leaf by leaf as required. These last for weeks.

You can plan to have lettuces all the year round but it is not often that amateurs can produce really good hearted lettuces in the winter. Some are hardier than others as we shall see, but if you aim to produce some under cloches for winter, may I suggest that you be prepared to pull some younger than you would in summer to give you leaves for salads rather than hearts. This way you can easily stretch the season. Grand Rapids, mentioned above, can be grown as a pot plant in a greenhouse where there is a little heat, or even on a sunny window sill in the house.

Most of us tend to have a favourite variety of lettuce, but nevertheless I suggest that it is often wisest to grow two varieties or even more, rather than to concentrate on only one. This way you are almost sure of a good crop no matter what the season. To have lettuce for cutting in late May until August and onwards, the seeds should be sown in spring and summer outdoors, from March until early August. All the varieties suitable for this purpose can be grown in succession to give you an unbroken supply. The trick is to sow a new row as soon as you see the seed leaves of the previous row appear above the soil. Those which germinate at the end of summer will go on into October and even later. I reckon to have crisp Webbs Wonderful to pick from cloches in November. You can use the same varieties throughout this time if you sow just a little at a time.

You can steal a march by sowing some of the seed in boxes to go into a cold greenhouse or a cold frame, even indoors on a window sill, in January and February and then plant the seedlings under cloches. Alternatively sow them in soil under cloches in March and thin these out. I find that this really is worth while, especially when the spring is cold. Seedlings can be transplanted from a cloche row, and these will of course be later than those which were not disturbed. If a row of seed is then sown in the open ground at the end of the month, your succession will be well under way. Some varieties are better suited for this early sowing than others. Suttons Unrivalled is an example.

There is such variety among lettuces that if you have a special type of soil or are in a particular locality you are likely to be able to find one which will do better with you than any other. It is worth while asking your seedsman or studying a seed catalogue, or perhaps a neighbour or the local horticultural society will have advice for you. Suttons, for instance, suggest that Windermere, which is one of the Great Lakes type, is ideal for growing in hot, dry conditions. In fact most of the crisphead varieties do well in hot, dry summers. Even so, I should point out that all summer lettuce grow best in the shade of some other crop, so try to grow them on the side away from the hot sun. As all rows should run from south to north, lettuce planted on the eastern side of a row of peas, for example, should benefit from their shade.

As I said earlier, although we talk of winter lettuce, actually there are not many occasions when we can pick a really good hearted lettuce in the depths of winter. There are varieties which can be grown in a heated greenhouse and others which can be grown in warmed frames, but I do not think that these are crops for the beginner. Much depends upon the season and the amount of shelter and protection you can give the plants as well as the nature of your soil.

If you have a warm, south-facing border you can grow lettuces to see you through the winter without protection, unless the season proves to be an unusually severe one. Sow seed in late August or early September for this purpose.

If at the end of autumn you still have some good lettuce plants growing outdoors but have no cloches to cover them until you need them, it is possible to transplant them into a frame, even a temporary one made just for this purpose. Lift them with a really good root mass and plant them in moist peat close together but not quite touching.

Growth is relatively slow in late autumn, winter and early spring, and I find it enough to continue thinning alternate plants so that I gradually pull slightly larger plants than last time. Meanwhile the space between the plants gradually widens until by the time they begin to make hearts they are well spaced.

Often plants which have remained sluggish during the winter heart up beautifully when the longer days come, and of course from the home economics point of view these are just as valuable.

Varieties which are sown in autumn to 'head up' in spring are not suitable for spring or summer sowing, so you need more than one variety if you want to stretch the crop over the year. On the other hand some cos varieties such as Lobjoits Green Cos can be sown in spring and autumn.

For the so-called winter lettuce you should sow seed in August and September. Imperial Winter, Valdor and Arctic King are good varieties for sowing in the open ground, and as you would expect, they are that little bit finer if they are covered by cloches.

A good cos variety which has been popular for many years is the dwarf, compact Winter Density, and this also can be sown in spring and early summer. So if you have seed left it need not be wasted.

If you have only a small plot you may consider sowing Mixed Lettuce. Seedsmen now make up a mixture of cabbage and cos varieties which though sown at the same time will mature at different dates. These should be sown in succession just like the unmixed varieties, from March to mid-July. I have tried these and find them good. They have one particular appeal, you have a chance of tasting several different varieties, and it is interesting to discover how they differ in flavour, texture and size.

Seed should always be sown thinly in shallow drills and rows should be 12ins apart. Thin as soon as you can, because if you let lettuce remain very crowded botrytis is likely to set in and rot the plants.

Marrows (*including courgettes or zuccini, pumpkin and squash*)
The humble though often giant marrow has for long been a feature of our gardens and allotments. Generally in the past it was not cut until it was really large, with the consequence that when cooked it was dull and insipid. No wonder that there was once such a spate of marrow and ginger jam and mustard pickle making at the end of the year. Something had to be used to give it flavour and to use up the usual annual bounty. Fortunately tastes have changed and apart from eating our marrows younger and finding them quite palatable after all, we are accepting and even seeking other varieties of vegetables from the same family.

If you have only tasted giant marrows, do try them young, for they are much more interesting and what is more they are easier to prepare since none of them need be wasted. Like squash they can be cooked with their skins and centres. This tender-seeded portion is not pithy in young fruits and in fact it improves the flavour and texture.

Courgettes are baby marrows, but of a special type. The varieties have been bred and selected to produce many female flowers so that the tiny fruits continue to be produced. These are best gathered as soon as the faded bloom drops naturally from the end of the fruit. But their fruits may, like those of the other varieties, be left to grow large and ripe. In fact I know one gardener, who for some reason known only to himself, never gathers them when they are small. If you want a few fruits to store for winter, simply leave one on each plant to mature, and continue cutting the others which form as soon as they are large enough.

Squash, which you will find grouped under the heading of marrow in most seed catalogues with the name squash probably left out altogether, is another form of gourd which varies considerably in size and appearance. Obviously seedsmen list only those varieties which can be expected to mature in our short summer season. If you can grow pumpkins, another form of squash, you should be able to grow those squash offered by the seedsmen. There are summer and winter squashes. The former are best cooked young and I would say that where you can grow courgettes you can grow summer squash.

Generally our old marrow is either Long Green Trailing, Green Bush,

Long White Trailing or White Bush. Custard Marrow is a squash, which for some reason has been more favourably accepted by the old-time gardeners and has been grown in our gardens for a long time. Americans call it Yellow Bush Scallop Squash or Pattypan Squash, both names on account of its shape.

From my point of view these edible gourds, of any variety, are among the most profitable of our garden crops. They vary considerably in taste, texture, size and shape. If you grow, say, Golden Courgette, you would have a delicious vegetable for salads, for it is beautifully nutty when raw as well as when cooked. Its texture and flavour would be very different from, say, Golden Delicious Squash, which is sweet and mealy when cooked and which will keep all winter, or Little Gem, eaten while still green, or Baby Crookneck, which also is best eaten young. It differs slightly from the others in colour and flavour. Vegetable Spaghetti will again give you something quite different from the others, for in this case the large fruit is boiled or baked whole, when the centres can be scooped out and eaten with pepper, salt and butter much like the pasta after which it is named.

Some of these are trailers, which means that they will also climb. Others make neat bush plants about the size of a courgette plant. Bush plants usually produce fruits earlier. You need only few plants of each for a small family. You can often find plants on sale, but I suggest that you grow your own and do a little swapping so as to get a selection of different varieties. My advice is to sow the seed where the plants are to grow. Give them warmth undersoil with lawn mowings, and glass above.

Give all of these plants good, rich soil. Prepare it in advance, making it warm and snug with plenty of humus, including fresh lawn mowings if you have them down below a topping of good soil.

You can raise the seeds in two ways. If you make the stations for the plants roughly on the hot bed system, you can sow the seeds in May directly where the plants are to remain, but they should be under cover and remain protected until early June. Since every seed cannot be expected to germinate, it is the practice to sow two or three to each station. If necessary you can then thin out, leaving two bush types or one trailer to each station. If there are surplus seedlings they can be transplanted if you wish, but they will of course mature a little later.

The other method is to sow the seeds singly in pots which should be stood in a heated frame, greenhouse or on a sunny window sill. Incidentally, always push the seed into the soil edgewise. Keep the plants moving. Repot them as soon as this appears necessary. You can plant them out under cloches at the end of April. Otherwise begin hardening them off in May, putting them outside on good days and bringing them indoors at nights.

Plant them outside during the first week in June and here again keep them moving. The earlier the plants flower the better the crop you will have. When you plant try to disturb the roots as little as possible. Follow my tip on first planting a flower pot given in the chapter on Personal Touches. Watch out for and guard against slugs.

The bush plants like an open sunny position. They really take up very little space. Reckon a little more than a square yard for each, and remember that if you prepare the soil well in advance you can use it meanwhile for a catch crop, radish perhaps, or it could serve as a nursery bed.

Trailing varieties take more room unless they are allowed or encouraged to climb. You can use these plants as screens or to cover any vertical surface, so long as they are well supported. If you have to let them trail on the ground you can keep them under control by guiding the trails in the direction you wish them to go and then inserting canes alongside to keep them in position. If they grow too long for your liking, pinch out the shoots. Do this also if the trails fail to branch. If there is plenty of space between them, you can direct them along between rows of potatoes or brassicas, but not between rows of low-growing or small plants.

Don't despair if at first the plants seem only to produce male flowers. This frequently happens and applies to all varieties. You can copy the Italians and use the flowers for cooking. Finally a day will come when many of the flowers are female, their petals rising from a tiny structure the shape of the particular fruit. It is wise to pollinate these flowers at the beginning of the season, otherwise you may find that many of them will abort. The operation is quite simple. Pick off a male flower and remove its petals. Brush its centre against the centre of the female flower. Then throw it away and pick another male flower for the next female. If the male flowers are open but not the females, you can sometimes hold them back for a few hours by picking them and putting the stems in water.

During the summer keep the marrow plants well watered. I like also to go over them morning and evening with clean water poured from a fine rose watering can to soak the leaves.

Any marrow required for storage should be left to mature and gathered just before the frosts. It really is a matter of watching the weather and listening to the weather reports. The riper the fruit, the better it will keep. Its skin should become wood hard. Do not be misled by the hard skin, but treat the fruits as though they were eggs. Neither bang them about nor damage the skin in any way. They should not be stored in a cold place, instead keep the temperature around 10–18°C (50–65°F).

Save all the net bags in which certain goods such as oranges and lemons are retailed, and use these to hang the marrows during storage. Otherwise simply lay them on a shelf or table, taking care not to lay them one on another. Use those with the softest skins first.

The easiest way to soften the skin is to place the marrow in a warm oven until it softens. You can then easily cut the skin.

Onions

Speak to any experienced gardener about onions and you are sure to uncover some personal foible in respect of this particular crop. There are
those who refuse to grow them on any but the same land year after year,
others who know exactly on what date they will sow seed, others who
favour sets rather than seeds, yet more who swear by transplanted seedlings from boxes raised in heat in January, some who are interested only
in 4lb bulbs, and many, many more, sharing a host of other beliefs and
dogmas. This could be inhibiting to a beginner, which would be a pity,
because it is perfectly possible to grow onions quite simply and with little
ceremony.

Perhaps because I am a cook first and a vegetable gardener second, I
have never been able to understand some of the attitudes towards this
vegetable, the sacredness of waiting until the spring-sown bulbs are ripe,
for example. I have known people with several rows of growing onions
in the garden who will go to town to buy imported bulbs rather than
gather immature roots of their own. This seems to me to be a shortsighted
policy. Food crops are surely grown to be eaten, and so long as they are
palatable and the action is not grossly wasteful I cannot see that it matters
overmuch at what point they are gathered, brought into the home and put
into the pot.

Considering the onion as a fresh rather than a stored vegetable might
help some gardeners to gain more value from their plots. There are some
lands on which it does not seem possible to raise good onions for store.
They will grow from sets but will not ripen properly, so why not grow a
crop from sets and pull them as soon as they have increased enough in
size to be useful for cooking and to have shown a profit? Tops can be used
as well as the bulbs.

Most people grow onions to store for the winter and spring. If these are
good, or if enough have been grown they might even go on until early
summer. To store well they must become thoroughly ripened bulbs. At the
same time as these are grown, other, smaller varieties are grown for pickling. These are usually harvested a little earlier than the large store types,
but not necessarily so. Then there are green onions, or spring or bunching
onions, grown for salad and sown in late August. They can be left in the
ground all winter. Usually the thinnings are used for salads and the spaced
plants allowed to remain and grow. They will produce good large bulbs,
but these will not keep for long and so they must be used in summer.

So if you want onions all year round and so long as your soil is suitable,
obviously it is best to grow two kinds, one to be started in the spring and
the other in late summer. I suggest that a beginner gardener plants some
onion sets in March to store for the coming winter, and as this is the first
year, to use some of these during the summer, and also to sow seed of one
of the new, very fast maturing Japanese varieties in August. These will
provide spring onions and large bulbs by the following July, which means

that the following year's store bulbs need not be used young as some were in the first season.

Onion sets are tiny onion bulbs produced from seed sown the previous year and sown thickly so that they would ripen prematurely. When these are planted they begin growing almost immediately. They soon shoot and the bulbs begin to swell. You can plant them as soon as you see the little bulbs on sale. Some are very small indeed and these as a whole do not grow well. They are usually sold by the pound and there should be something like 200 to the 1lb. They are sometimes packeted, but never buy any that you cannot inspect. They should be about ⅜ to ⅝ins in diameter.

When planting you can simply take a garden line as a guide and press the bulbs into the soil along this, but if you do you are likely to find them all strewn over the soil surface a day or two later, moved by the worms. It is much better to draw shallow drills just about as deep as the bulbs themselves. Push the bulbs into the soil at the bottom of this drill. I space mine quite closely, an inch or so apart, and then, as I said earlier, I pull alternate plants once my winter stored bulbs are used. If I have plenty in store I space them further apart when I begin planting.

Sometimes these plants begin to flower, depending on the season. If you do not want to pull up and use the plant, take off the top of the flowering stem. The plant will then form a smaller bulb or two at the base of the flowering stem.

Onions prefer a light or medium soil. They will not grow well on heavy soils, nor on those which are very light, on clay or chalk. Like beans, you can grow them on the same soil year after year, so it might pay you to concentrate on one area and bring its soil to the perfect state for this crop. My own grow in a new place each year. I like to dress the soil with lime in early February and then give it another light dusting before I plant sets or sow the seed. Onion seed grows best in soil which has been well firmed.

March and April are the usual spring months for sowing seeds, but sometimes you can sow them at the end of February if the season is favourable. From this time onwards take every advantage that a fine day offers to prepare the soil. It should have a fine tilth. If the soil is to be firmed it must be dry. Do not attempt to work on it if the soil sticks to the soles of your shoes. Even though it helps so much to have an early start, do not be in a hurry to get the seed in the soil until you are quite sure that it is in the right condition. Draw shallow drills 9ins apart and sow the seed very thinly. Cover and re-firm the soil by treading it lightly.

You can grow good medium-sized onions by spacing the plants 2ins apart. You can transplant thinnings if you wish. If you have some gaps in the row use these to fill in the spaces. Alternatively, use them to make another row elsewhere. These would give you some onions to pull in summer should you want them. Or you can simply pull the onions from time to time for use in salads or in cooking, spacing them as you go.

Onions suffer from the attentions of a beastly little pest called the onion fly. Loose soil lightens her labour, so see that you leave no young roots open to attack. After you have pulled out an onion seedling or a weed from among the plants, do not leave a hole in the soil or loose earth around the onion roots. Make the soil firm again by pressing it down with your fingers or foot. One of the advantages of sowing early is that you can evade attack because the plants get well ahead and are too old to attract the fly by the time she appears on the scene. Onions grown from sets also escape onion fly trouble.

If you want to grow onions for pickling, choose one of the special quick maturing varieties such as the well tried Paris Silver Skin or the newer Barletta Barla, which can be harvested by July if you sow the seed in April. Most of them take about 12 weeks to mature, and you can sow the seed at any time from March to July. Make the drills a little wider than for the large onions and sow the seed thickly so that the plants will jostle each other in the rows. This crowding also helps them to mature quicker.

If you are not really very concerned about having large onions in the kitchen, you might consider growing plenty of these little onions, so prized by French cooks, for cooking rather than for pickling. They are so easy to grow, and once you have tasted them you are unlikely to crave for the four pounders.

As the onion plants grow tall, avoid bending their tops as you work or walk along the row. However, by the end of August should they all still be standing erect, make a special point of bending them over, for this will help the bulbs to ripen. Bend the tops over on the shady side of the bulb so that their tips rest on the soil, thus exposing a large portion of the bulb to sunlight.

In September lift the onions. They are ready for lifting when the tops are no longer green but have died down to a little brown tail. Lifted before this they will not store well. Do not knock them or throw them about, for if they are bruised they will not keep but will turn rotten. After you have lifted the bulbs lie them in the sun, or in the air, to ripen and dry thoroughly.

Bring the bulbs indoors for the winter. First clean them by rubbing off loose skins and roots. Do not pull off the 'tunics', simply pull away any skin which is obviously loose and dirty.

The simplest and I think the best way of storing them is to put them in net bags and hang them in a dry but not sunny place.

Parsnips
Parsnips are often so cheap in the shops that you may wonder if they are worth growing. The only thing I can say to influence you is that the taste of a newly lifted root is far superior to that of one that has been in a greengrocer's shop or on a supermarket shelf for several days.

There are not many varieties of parsnips in cultivation, but there is a good new one which has thicker, shorter roots than the traditional long, tapering type. The new one is called Avonresister and was bred by the National Vegetable Research Station. It grows well everywhere and is said to be especially good on shallow soils. This is a great improvement, since parsnips generally have to be grown on deep soil. This should not be freshly manured though, or the roots will become forked and fanged. In some districts parsnips can be sown in February, but there is a danger here, because should the season turn wet and cold the parsnips tend to develop root canker. It is best to wait until the soil is warm and dry, and for a windless day. Although the seed is large it is so light that it will be whirled up and away from one end of the drill before you can reach the other. Actually you can sow parsnips at any time from March to May. The crop takes from 24 to 27 weeks to mature. Usually the roots are not lifted until after the first frosts because they are then said to be better flavoured. There is no other reason why you should not lift them earlier. I have done so when I have wanted the vegetable to use in a casserole.

You can also sow seed in July. This usually germinates more quickly than the spring sown. As you would expect, the roots do not reach a great size before winter. They are intended to be eaten as young roots and they are succulent and delicious. It is worth while growing them if you have the space to spare or some seed left over from spring. Parsnip seed does not remain viable for long.

The seeds are large enough to handle separately and I used to follow the recommended practice of sowing groups of five seeds at 9in intervals in drills 1in deep, but quite frankly I found this a fiddling waste of time. There is always so much more seed than one requires in a packet that I find it suits me best merely to sprinkle the seeds along the drill as one does with most other crops, and then to thin out later.

Parsnip plants grow quite handsomely with very large leaves, so we have to provide adequate space for them. Even so I think that 9ins is rather too wide a space for the small garden. From any time after the little plants are large enough to handle, that is when one true leaf appears, thin them out so that you have a row of singly spaced plants quite close together. Leave them for a week or two and then go over them again, leaving the biggest plants wherever possible until they are from 4 to 8ins apart. It really depends on whether you like giant or medium-sized roots. Keep the rows weeded when the plants are young.

As the parsnips take so long to germinate you can sow radish with them. Be sure to pull these as soon as they are ready. By this time the parsnip seedlings should be ready for thinning out.

As I said earlier, the parsnips sown in July should be pulled as soon as they are large enough to use and not left until they are old, unless, that is, you have not sown any seed in the spring. Those plants which were sown in the early part of the year should be saved for winter use. They may be left in the ground all winter and lifted as required. Personally I think that they are best this way, but of course there are problems if or when the soil becomes frosted, so it is often wise to lift and store a few, like carrots, for such an eventuality.

If there are any roots left in the ground by the following March you should lift them or they will begin to grow again. I find that it helps me considerably to freeze these last few, for then I have the roots to use during spring and early summer, at which time root vegetables are often difficult to find.

Peas

If you study a seed catalogue you will see that the garden peas are mainly divided into three groups, the Earlies, the Second Earlies and the Maincrop varieties. Generally speaking the first are ready for picking after 12 weeks and can be coaxed into early production by sowing them early, i.e., at the end of the year, and giving them cloche protection. The second earlies take a week or two longer to mature and are sown in March and April. The maincrops take about a week longer still, i.e., 13 to 14 weeks. As these should be sown during March and April, you can see that they will come into production during July and August. You can also see that they will be occupying garden space for a considerable period.

It is possible with skill and good planning, combined with luck and good weather, to have peas by the end of May and to carry on with them to the end of summer. However, for the new gardener there are certain drawbacks to be considered, and although I am always willing to have a gamble so far as a vegetable crop is concerned, it would not be honest of me if I did not point these out. But I must say that my own fresh garden peas bring me so much pleasure and satisfaction that I would urge everyone to grow some. You can always begin in a small way and extend if you think it worth while.

The first early varieties are usually the most rewarding simply because if they are sown outdoors in March or April they are grown at a time of the year when the weather conditions suit them. In a normal year they begin in the rainy season and they flower when the sun shines and the days are warmer. Summer droughts and wet, cold summers are both detrimental to the pea crop and these affect most the later-maturing varieties. Drought is particularly deadly and sometimes there are dramatic failures among some maincrop varieties grown in areas where the soil dries out badly. Do not attempt to grow these unless you are certain that the soil is deep and rich in humus so that it retains water, and also that you can generously mulch the plants to keep them cool at the roots. I firmly believe that the liberal mulchings of lawn mowings I use are responsible for the good pea crops, but of course in a really dry season there will also be a lack of these, and in this case mulchings of well rotted compost will help to shade the roots and to keep the moisture in the soil.

If you fear that this might be the case in your own garden, yet you are hoping to harvest a good crop of peas for freezing, may I suggest that you forget about successional cropping and raise all you want at one season from the first or second earlies. You will find that there are some very good varieties among them suitable for freezing.

The other drawback is that most peas, even some of the dwarf varieties, grow and crop better when they are supported. Some will grow quite well without sticks, Feltham First is an example, yet even here supports are an advantage, for I think you will find they take up much less space if they are kept upright, and in small gardens this is one of the more important considerations.

At one time it used to be easy to find pea sticks and relatively cheap to buy them. This is not so today. However, there are other, cheaper, though not necessarily less laborious ways of supporting peas and I describe some of them in my chapter on Personal Touches.

Yet another drawback is that several rows of peas can take up quite a lot of space. One or two rows can usually be fitted in to a small garden quite conveniently, but when you consider that some varieties which are highly recommended for freezing can grow as tall as 5ft, you can see that considerable space should be afforded them. You can use the rows as screens of course, or you can use the tripod method as recommended for runner beans.

If you plan to grow more than one row of peas you should reckon to keep the distance between the rows roughly equal to their height, e.g., 5ft high peas and 5ft between the rows. During the early part of the year this space can be used for quick maturing crops such as radishes and lettuces, which will appreciate the shade and possibly the shelter from the sticks, and in late summer you can allow trailing marrows to make their way along the rows. Plant these some 5ft from the peas and then point the trails in the right direction. If you have only one row, naturally other plants need not be placed 5ft away from the peas. They can go quite close.

Some soils produce better pea crops than others. They do not usually do well on very limy soils, although you can, like me, provide them with plenty of humus to make the soil more acid. I like to use plenty of peat in the drills when I sow the seed, and as I said earlier, I believe in mulching them generously. Peas also like deep soil, they are not surface rooting, and their roots go down a long way searching for food as well as moisture. For this reason, according to your method of gardening, you should either deeply dig and manure the ground in preparation for the crop or you should grow them on ground from which you have previously lifted some deep growing roots such as parsnips. This is what I do. It is also advisable to move the crop around so that the rows occupy a new site each year. There are some gardeners who maintain that a pea crop should not be grown in the same soil more than once in five years.

Now a word about the peas themselves. There are two main kinds, round and wrinkled seeded, the first being hardier than the second. The wrinkled peas are also called marrowfat, and they are sweeter. Round peas are also to be found in Petit Pois, Mangetout or Sugar Peas and the attractively coloured Purple Podded Pea.

I have grown the sugar peas for many years now and I find them an extremely profitable crop. Cooked whole, as they are meant to be, they are as sweet as any marrowfat and there is no waste. Simply top and tail them. As you do this the 'string' which surrounds the joint of the pods is pulled away at the same time. They vary in height from 3 to 5ft according to variety. I find that they crop heavily and they freeze quite well.

I have grown the tall Purple Podded peas because they are pretty and I have been rewarded with quite large crops of large pods which were always full. The pea seeds are green. I found that even if you pick them young, they tend to be mealy, mealier than other round-seeded varieties. All the same they make excellent green pea soup. The plants look attractive grown up tripods in the flower garden. They will also climb a wire netting fence prettily.

Petit Pois, 3ft tall, is very hardy. Although the individual peas are very small, the plants carry a heavy crop of pods and so this variety is well worth growing. Although it does not have quite the style of the Petit Pois, the better known and more widely grown Little Marvel, 20ins tall, is much like it in size and taste and is one of the heaviest croppers there is. It has been around for a long time but still takes some beating.

Varieties of peas are numerous. Each year sees its novelty introduction, and I seem to have spent many long days with other gardening writers walking along rows of new peas which seemed to stretch off to the horizon, while the seedsman pointed out to us their undoubted qualities.

Old and tried varieties of peas tend to remain on the scene mainly I suspect because gardeners are conservative and having once found a variety which does well with them are reluctant to change, yet some of the new varieties are very good indeed and I like to try one each year. A great deal of time and research goes into their hybridisation and none is marketed unless it really is an improvement on those that have gone before in some way or another. An example is Sweetness, bred by Suttons, the first wrinkled seeded pea to mature as early as the round seeded. It is also a heavy cropper and a good freezer. Many varieties are being bred with the freezer in mind. So rather than just picking up any packet of peas from the display stand or counter, try to study a catalogue so that you can find a variety or some varieties which you believe will suit your circumstances and your needs best. There is sure to be one.

If you decide to have a go with sowing peas in November and keeping them snug under cloches for the winter, you will need a dwarf early variety. There are some more suitable for this purpose than others. Obviously really dwarf varieties are necessary mainly because you do not want to have to remove the cloches to give them head room at the very time when there are severe frosts, for pea blossom can be killed by frost. There are Meteor, 12ins, Unwins Mini, 12ins, and Feltham First, 18ins, for example.

If you live in a warm district or if you have a sheltered garden or a warm border you can sow the hardy early varieties in the open ground in November. Watch for their germination and get them supported as early as you can, preferably with twigs because these will help protect them. I have one gardener friend who is a firm believer in letting weeds grow around these and autumn-sown onions because he declares that the weeds help to protect the cultivated plants. He says that they do not take long to clear in the spring. I prefer to use a mulch of well rotted humus. Watch out for slugs.

It is usually more convenient to sow peas in double or even treble rows with the seeds 3ins apart each way. It takes time and is often a little weary-ing, but it is worth while to sow the seeds individually. Apart from any-thing else it helps to make a packet of seed go much further. A ½pt of seed should sow a 30ft row. The drill should be 3ins deep. As I said earlier, I like to make a deep drill and to line it well with peat. This is moistened to aid germination. The seeds are then laid on it. They are covered with soil, or if the soil is very limy with more moistened peat and then soil.

In some areas and in some seasons mice are a nuisance. Actually I like wild mice, but I cannot afford to have my vegetable seeds eaten, so I find it necessary to set traps.

Wait until the pea seedlings are through the ground before supporting the pea plants.

Asparagus peas. Once I learned about these I could not wait to try them. Now I do not grow them every year, but from time to time. They make an interesting change to one's diet and they are pretty little plants.

The name is very descriptive because the pods really do taste like asparagus, but unless you know about them eating the peas can be a disaster rather than a pleasant gastronomic experience. It is essential that you pick the seed pods while they are very young. This should be not long after the flower has faded. If you leave them to grow large, eating them will be a little like eating bony fish.

If you have only a few plants, pick them over daily and put the pods in the refrigerator until you have gathered enough for a meal.

The plant is not a true pea. It is an annual, *Tetragonolobus purpureus*, and it is attractive enough for it to be grown sometimes for the sake of its pretty little deep red flowers.

Grow the plants in rows across the vegetable patch, in groups in a flower border, or as an edging along the side of a path. Space them 6 to 12ins apart. Support them while they are quite young if you do not wish them to sprawl. Sow the seeds individually where the plants are to flower.

Potatoes

Like allotments, the popularity of potatoes is in direct proportion to the hardness of the times. In good days comparatively few potatoes are grown in gardens and allotments. Now the demand for both is on the increase.

Of recent years there has been such a small demand for potato seed that some seedsmen and other suppliers have decreased their stocks to such an extent that it is now difficult to find certain varieties. It is hard now to realise that there was a time when an exhibit of potatoes at one of the Royal Horticultural Society shows would fill several yards of staging, or that there would be shown in it tubers which varied not only in shape and size but in colour too, from near white to violet-black, from golden yellow to bright rose.

Potatoes are divided for the gardener according to their season of maturity, into First Earlies, which are ready in late May or June; Second Earlies, ready in July and August; and Late or Maincrop, which mature in September and October. There are kidney shaped and round tubers as well as a few special kinds such as the elongated Fir Apple Pink, a potato which is known also as a salad potato because it is delicious first boiled and then eaten cold in salads. There is also Jaune d'Hollande, a yellow fleshed variety, small and not a heavy cropper, but with a waxy texture and a subtle, delicate and haunting flavour that has made it the delight of gourmets.

Potatoes can be planted from February and mid-March in the south to mid-April in the north. You will need about 40 tubers for a 50ft row. This is roughly 7lbs but will depend upon the variety. Most people like to grow a few earlies because their flavour is so good, a considerable quantity of the maincrop because these will feed the family for most of the year, and then a few lates to eke out the supply until the earlies come round again.

Always try to get certified seed, which is virus-free and may save you a lot of trouble. Never keep your own seed potatoes, for by doing so you will save very little money and risk losing an entire crop. It is wise also to grow only varieties which are immune to wart disease. Immune earlies include Home Guard (crops well, good flavour), Ulster Chieftan and Arran Pilot (heavy cropper). Maincrops include Arran Banner (good quality, huge cropper), Desirée (good cooker), Majestic (most popular heavy cropper) and Marus Piper (early maincrop, good cooker, rarely discolours) and for the lates Pentland Crown is a good immune variety.

Wart disease is notifiable, which means that if you find it in your crop (you can't mistake it) you *must* report it to the Ministry of Agriculture. The disease is so serious that a year or two ago there was a complete ban on the growing by amateur growers of susceptible varieties, which include such popular types as Epicure, King Edward, and Sharpes Express, and it was largely because of the outcry that followed that the ban was removed. Other diseases are less dramatic, but in a wet season beware of blight and avoid it by spraying your crop with Bordeaux mixture in about mid-June to mid-July. Never grow potatoes in exactly the same spot in successive years. If possible always allow at least two years to elapse.

Buy seed potatoes early in the season. They are called sets or seed. The potato is an underground stem. If you examine it carefully you will notice that all the 'eyes' (really buds) are at one end of the tuber, or mainly so. These buds should be encouraged to shoot while they are still out of the soil, so that once they are planted they will grow ahead.

Seed tubers should be laid out in February so that the eyes can develop. They may be stood in shallow boxes or in trays in a cool place which is both light and frostproof. Stand the tubers on end, eye ends uppermost.

Before you plant make your soil really rich and productive. If it is either heavy or light, condition it with lots of strawy manure or with hop manure. Dig this in well. For the best possible crop add a good, rich, specialised potato fertiliser with plenty of potash. Do not add lime unless your soil is excessively acid, but if there is any left from previous applications it will give your potatoes an extra floury texture. Use no other forms of artificial fertiliser as they can harm your crop.

Begin planting when the soil is moist but not sticky, when the weather is brightening and the days begin to look a bit better. Start with your earlies and carry on through the maincrop and the lates, not worrying too much about the actual date.

A most thorough way to ensure a good crop is to dig trenches for each row about 5ins deep and place the potatoes in these at the correct intervals. Sprinkle a little fresh grass mowings over the potatoes to prevent scab and then cover with rich soil.

If time counts or if you are later in the season than you would like, use a garden line and with a trowel or spade dig a hole every 1ft for the earlies and 3ins more for the maincrop and lates. Place the potatoes carefully in these holes with the main shoots or eyes pointing upwards and then cover them in. Rows should be about 2½ft apart.

If your soil is really weedy and overgrown your potatoes can help you clear it. There are two main ways and the easiest but more expensive is to use Weedol as already suggested. But on the other hand you can just ignore the weeds, dig your holes and plant in spite of them. As the potatoes grow you will have to earth them up by hoeing the soil up to the main stems and in this way you will also be clearing the weeds. Then finally, when you actually dig your fully grown crop, you will expose all the weeds and their long or deep roots, and at this point you can pull them up and burn them, leaving your patch of soil ready dug and weeded for your next crop.

As soon as some of the first growth from your newly planted potatoes appears above the soil surface, cover this little fuzz of green with soil. This will help to protect it in case of a late frost. Then, when it grows through once again, merely pull up the soil on each side of the row with a hoe to leave just the tops showing. Carry on earthing up like this, though perhaps not so drastically, until the plants are fully grown. This holds the plants upright and supports them, it gives a greater depth of soil for the plant and hence more space for the actual tubers to grow and get fat, and it gives you a little more space to move along your crop.

There is still another way you can grow your potatoes and this does away with any digging at all. Just lay your potatoes on the ground at the correct spacing in your straight rows, preferably just pressing them lightly into the soil to keep the growing top uppermost. Among them sprinkle some slug pellets to kill any of these pests that may appear. Then cover the rows with strips of black plastic sheeting, available especially for this purpose and quite cheap from all good garden stores. Weight this down at the edges and ends by piling a little soil on at these places. After a while you will notice that the potatoes have started to grow and are pushing against the underside of the sheeting. At these places take a sharp knife and merely cut a little cross in the plastic so that the plants can push through and grow upwards but so that no light can get beneath the plastic to the potatoes underneath. The young potatoes will grow there quite happily, and when they are due for gathering all you need do is lift one end of the plastic and pick up the best of those within reach and then weight down the cover again so that the others can continue to grow just as they had been doing.

But let's face it, the reason why most people still grow potatoes the old way is because it's the best way, giving you more and better potatoes, and this is a crop that can well be uneconomic unless you do well with it. They normally take about four months to mature. Feed them with a special potash-rich potato fertiliser at least once in this time, preferably twice. Spray them in mid-June to mid-July against blight. Do this every ten days or fortnight, especially if the weather is wet.

You should end up with from six to eight times the weight of your seed, not a bad dividend.

Radish

Possibly it is because members of my family seem to have such a passion for radishes that I find myself preoccupied with raising them for as many months as I can. Unfortunately it is one variety, French Breakfast, that seems to be the most popular, although of recent years the long tapering White Icicle has found more favour. There are several other varieties, some of which mature quicker than others. As I have described in the chapter on Personal Touches, I grow many of my radishes along with other crops, but this applies only to the oval-rooted French Breakfast.

When considering what variety to grow, remember that the long-rooted varieties do best when sown in spring and the round or oval ones do better in summer. Besides the red and white summer varieties there are others which may be grown as a winter vegetable. These should be sown in the autumn and they should be thinned out as soon as possible to 6 to 9ins apart, otherwise they will not make good roots but will instead produce more green tops than root. These winter radish include the Round Black Spanish, Long Black Spanish and China Rose. All of these grow really quite large and should be sliced or grated when served.

The most important thing about cultivating radish is to ensure that they can grow quickly. They will then be plump and succulent. This means that soil should be rich and that the plants must never suffer from drought. Since I began using peat enriched with a little balanced fertiliser in the drills whenever I sowed radish, I have improved considerably the quality of my crop.

You can begin sowing seeds of the summer varieties outdoors as early as February if you have some warm, sheltered spot which faces south and you can use this same site for the last sowing of the same kinds. To ensure a succession you can sow fortnightly from this time until October, changing the site according to the season. The radishes should reach maturity in 5 to 6 weeks. If you use cloches you can begin sowing them earlier still, from January to March if you live in the south or from February in the colder north.

If you want to use the whole width of a cloche you should be able to sow five rows. There may also be some space alongside some other crop already covered by other cloches into which you could fit a row. It is possible sometimes to sow a row or more between two rows of cloches and here the 'valley' between them is often protected and warm.

Radishes often fail in the summer because they are in full sun. This makes them small and tough. Once you begin sowing seed for radish which will mature after midsummer, you should try to site the rows where the plants will keep cool and moist and where they can enjoy the benefit of the shade cast by taller vegetables, peas and beans for example. Sow the seeds on the shady side. Indeed, shade is so important in hot summers that it used to be the practice in some large private gardens to sow some seed in shady frames so that the radishes would not suffer from drought.

Sow the seed in drills 1in deep, and if you make several rows space them 6ins apart. The seed is large and it should not be difficult to sow it thinly. If you find that the seedlings grow thickly, thin them out as soon as you can handle them, even if this is only an inch apart. This will prevent the plants from growing lank and spindly.

Salsify and Scorzonera

Once you have eaten these delicious root vegetables I feel sure that you will want always to find some space for them in the kitchen garden. The roots are in season from mid-October through the winter until spring. If you care to leave some roots of salsify in the soil all winter they will shoot in the spring and you can use the 'chards' like cardoons, i.e., in salads or to cook.

The soil for both should be deep and rich. The site should be sunny and open. Usual practice is to sow the seeds in groups of three 9 to 12ins apart (scorzonera grows larger) in shallow drills in early April. When the seedlings have reached about 3ins high, thin them out leaving the largest to grow on.

Little more cultivation is necessary except that the flower heads should be picked off as they appear.

Lift the roots in November and store. First twist off the leaves and allow the roots to dry in the air. Then store them in boxes of dry sand or peat in the way recommended for carrots.

Shallots

There are two kinds of shallots in cultivation, the yellow-skinned and the red-skinned. Yellow shallots are not so strongly flavoured and they keep better in store. I like to grow both kinds because I think that the red have a more distinctive flavour.

In the chapter on Personal Touches I have described how I grow shallots during many months of the year. Here it should suffice to give general cultivation directions.

The 'seeds' which are individual bulbs are planted in much the same way as onion sets. You are often told that they can be merely pressed into the soil, but if this is done they can be pulled out of place by worms. It is best to make a slight depression for each bulb and cover it lightly with soil. This can be drawn away later if you find this necessary. Usually though the bulb pulls itself up from the soil as it grows.

Shallots can be planted in winter, but more generally they are planted in March. If you want them early make two or three plantings, beginning with one on the shortest day, and planting these in a warmer site than those you put out later in the season.

Grown well these bulbs should multiply. Wait until the foliage dies right down before you lift them. Let them dry in the sun and air. Clean them as recommended for onions and store in string bags away from frost and damp. Set aside some small, sound bulbs for next year's seed.

Spinach (see also Beetroot)

There are two kinds of the true spinach, the round-seeded or summer and the prickly-seeded or winter. Both kinds do best in rich soils containing ample humus.

Summer spinach tends to bolt if it is on poor land. You can eat the young flowering shoots, of course, along with the leaves, but these are a poor reward for all your labour. Once the plant flowers or even attempts to flower, pick out the shoots as soon as you see them. It is never quite so productive, nor do its leaves grow as large as when it holds back its flowers.

A whole long row of spinach may seem a great deal of vegetable, but as spinach lovers will know, even a two gallon bucketful of leaves cooks down to barely enough for a small family. Furthermore, once you begin to pick summer spinach it does not usually last much longer than three weeks or a month at most. Fortunately this is a vegetable which responds well to successional sowing. Reckon on it taking 9 to 11 months to grow to maturity. You can begin sowing the seeds of summer spinach at the end of February if the weather is fair, and carry on until the end of May.

This kind prefers a moist soil and drought will also cause the plants to bolt. Like radish it does best in the shade of taller plants. If you sow more than one row, summer spinach can go quite close, 9 to 12ins. Drills should be about 1in deep. Begin thinning when the plants are about 3ins high, just spacing them so that each individual stands alone, then thin them again when the plants begin to touch each other and continue until they are spaced about 6ins apart.

Winter spinach does best on moderately dry soil, so try to find it a well drained situation. One has to take into account that it is likely to receive sufficient moisture from the skies during its season. Sow the seed from July and September, as early as you can to give the seedlings a better start. It needs a little more space, so set rows 12–15ins apart.

After you have taken the thinnings begin gathering the leaves from the main plants. Be selective and take only a few leaves from each. If you strip a plant it will take a very long time to recover. You get more value from the crop by taking few leaves but often. Try to nip or cut off the leaves only. If you let the stems remain on the plant they will help to maintain it.

Sprouting crops – *at all times of the year*
Mustard and cress and bean shoots will be familiar to most people, but there are other seeds which can also be germinated easily and whose young shoots or sprouts provide valuable food crops rich in vitamins and proteins. The easiest to sprout are alfalfa, mung beans and fenugreek. Soy beans, sunflower, and the cereals oats, wheat, and rye, can also be treated this way. I understand that the seedsmen Thompson and Morgan hope soon to add more of this type of vegetable to their lists.

The amount you grow at a time will obviously depend on how much you want to use at a time, but as a guide, approximately a ½oz of seed will develop into 5–8oz of shoots off any of them. If necessary, harvested shoots can be put into plastic bags or cartons and kept in the refrigerator for two or three days. They can also be deep frozen.

Seeds should be grown in a dark, warm, moist atmosphere. You can sprout them in saucers, shallow bowls or seed trays on flannel or tissues kept moist in the same way as recommended for mustard and cress, but I think the following method is a better one. First soak the seed overnight, then put your original ½oz of seed (now heavier) into a wide mouthed 2lb jam jar and cover the end of the jar with muslin, a single piece of tissue or some other material which is not airtight. Lay the jar on its side so that the seed lies along the length of the jar. Keep it in a warm place such as an airing cupboard or covered with a cloth above a radiator. Once a day rinse the seeds with tepid water. Swish the water around very gently and then drain it off through the cloth over the mouth. (You can pour the water through the cloth into the jar.) Drain thoroughly each time because water left in the jar would cause the seeds to rot.

When the sprouts have grown (usually between 3–5 days) stand the jars in sunlight for several hours to give the seedlings an opportunity to make a little chlorophyll, for they will then be richer in vitamin C.

Sweet corn

At one time I would have hesitated to suggest that sweet corn, or maize, is a crop for the new gardener, but now, thanks to the hybridists, I can do this without hesitation. Today's varieties are a great improvement on the old types. They are not so tall, they mature faster, they will grow under cooler conditions and they have sweeter kernels.

No special soil is needed so long as it is in good heart. It should not be freshly manured, because this would lead to the production of too much foliage and not enough flower. Simply prepare it by dressing it with a balanced fertiliser.

Wind is a nuisance and in high winds plants tend to keel over, so if possible they should be protected in some way. On the other hand, gentle winds play an important part, for they help to pollinate the flowers, and to aid this process sweet corn plants should be placed in blocks rather than single rows. Plant them 12ins apart with 2ft between the rows.

Even though varieties mature faster than they used to do, it is still important to get the seed in early, and it will not germinate without warmth and protection. You can either sow the seeds in heat indoors in April, or outdoors under cover and in warm soil in May. Although indoors the seeds germinate quickly and the plants soon grow apace, they do receive a considerable check when they are transplanted. The difficulty usually is that the roots fill their small pots so quickly that the knocking out and transplanting damages them. There is less check if the seeds are sown in peat or soil blocks. It is prudent to sow two or three seeds to a station outdoors and then to thin them out later.

See that cloches are well closed and take care to make the soil warm with plenty of humus or lawn mowings. If you have no cloches use jars. These can be removed at the end of May when the frosts are over. The greatest trouble at the seed sowing stage comes from mice, who will also clear seeds from pots if they are able to get into the greenhouse.

It helps, to draw the soil up around the base of the stems of young plants, for this serves to anchor them. Later, when the plants have grown to 2 or 3ft, if you find that the site is more windy than you had realised, earth them up still further.

Tomatoes

How easy tomatoes are today! How encouraging that seedsmen are able to write, quite honestly, in a catalogue as Suttons do, 'Many varieties grow vigorously and bear heavy crops outdoors.' So if you have no greenhouse, go ahead and plan a row outdoors in some suitable place, but make sure that you plant a variety which has been bred for this purpose. You will often find tomato plants on sale, but you will also often find that these are unnamed and should therefore be viewed with some caution. Sometimes they will do well and sometimes not. It is so easy to raise your own plants on a window sill, and seed is so cheap, that I would suggest you study a seed catalogue to find the variety which would best suit your circumstances and then set about raising seed yourself. You are almost certain to raise too many plants, but think how good it will be to have some to pass on. Unless you are like my son, who has this year discovered the pleasures and economics of vegetable gardening for himself. He sowed one packet of tomatoes, putting one seed in each soil block, 53 seeds in all, and was so overcome when he discovered that every one had germinated that he planted them all. I imagine that we shall all be eating green tomato chutney for years to come!

The number of varieties of tomatoes is quite remarkable and in reading their descriptions you can see what points hybridists have had in mind when they crossed one with another, for there are those like the outdoor Bush Tomato types which need no staking nor pinching out of side shoots, and will grow well with little care. Tomatoes are usually grown on the cordon system, i.e., the centre stem is not allowed to branch. Those shoots which are not flowering stems and which grow in the axils of the main stem and leaves have to be pinched out as soon as they appear. This is not necessary with the bush kinds whose growth is allowed to develop naturally. The plants are allowed to sprawl on the ground. Like marrows you can guide them to grow which way you wish. Usually straw is placed on the ground under the fruits to keep them clean. You can also use plastic sheeting or those foamed plastic protective coats in which so many wine bottles travel today. Bush tomatoes include Outdoor Girl, Amateur, Histon Cropper, all of which are dwarf growing. There is even a variety suitable for flower pots or window boxes called Tiny Tim which grows only 15ins tall. Its fruits are also tiny, red currant like, but they taste good and they mature early. Those of the former varieties are normal sized.

Other than these bush types which are planted in the open ground, there are many which can also be grown in a border and which can even be grown in containers stood outdoors. These need to be staked and to have shoots pinched out. There is a great variety of choice, for apart from many excellent usual red varieties, there are, I think, splendid and very sweet yellow-skinned varieties such as Golden Queen and Yellow Perfection. There is also a yellow variety of the bush Amateur. If like me you prefer those great ugly fruits we buy on the continent, there is Marmande, which should only be grown outdoors. There are other whoppers such as Big Boy, but these are for growing under glass.

You can grow tomatoes in unheated greenhouses as well as outdoors, and usually the varieties suitable for a cold greenhouse can also be grown outdoors. A heated greenhouse can grow other varieties, but I do not intend to include greenhouse culture in this book.

I would recommend the absolute beginner to concentrate on outdoor tomatoes to begin with so that he or she gets to understand the crop a little. Plants grown under glass need a little more help. But just one important point: if you grow plants outdoors, and especially if you grow them in the open ground, do guard against potato blight. This will sometimes and in some seasons attack the plants and render them useless. This once happened to my plants. I had no idea that potato blight was so rife (there were fields of potatoes being grown on the farms around our garden) and I returned from holiday to find the plants too far gone to be able to do anything for them. It was very sad to have to destroy pounds and pounds of large green fruits. If someone nearby has had some trouble with potato blight at some time, or if the season turns damp and clammy, begin a proper routine of spraying with a copper or zinc based fungicide such as Bordeaux mixture, beginning early in July. This will not cost much and will be well worth while.

The seed for outdoor tomatoes need not be sown until March or early April because these are fast maturing varieties. Either sow them individually in peat or soil blocks or peat pots, or you can use small plastic pots. In spite of the slight extra work, I am sure that this is much the best method and quicker in the long run because you will not have to prick out the young plants. Even though they are in their own pots, keep an eye on the roots and if the pots get full, repot the plants. It is important to keep them growing. If the first flower truss forms, so much the better. During this time watch over and water the plants carefully so that they do not become too dry at the roots at any time.

Begin hardening them off on every possible occasion. Plant them outdoors during the first week in June in some warm and sheltered spot. Look around for a sun trap, they will not ripen well unless they are warm. See also that they are protected from strong winds which sometimes can blow the plants about and damage them. If the nights seem cold you can cover the plants with large inverted flower pots, but these must be removed as soon as it becomes light. Otherwise use cloches or if you have them, large glass jars.

Space out the plants 1½ to 2ft apart in the ground. Stake them at the same time that you plant them so that you do not damage the roots later. Do this adequately, remembering that plants which carry a good crop of fruit can become very heavy.

If the weather is moist, water the plants in their pots and let them drain before planting them. Make a hole deep enough so that the soil surface of the pot will sink about an inch below the new soil surface, but do not throw more earth over the root ball, simply see that the soil on all sides is touching it. Let it remain like this for a week or two unless the weather should become very dry. You will find that the roots will grow out from the ball into the surrounding soil quicker this way than if you cover them and water them in as is the practice with most other plants when they are transplanted or planted out.

What you should do, however, during this period and each day afterwards, is each morning to take a fine rose watering can or a garden spray and lightly damp the whole of the plant and the air immediately surrounding it. This helps the flowers to pollinate.

When the time comes, fill in the planting hole and mulch around the plants, leaving a little space around the stem so that the roots can be fed and watered. Once the first fruits have set, begin feeding the plants. Do this about once a fortnight using one of the proprietary tomato foods and following the directions faithfully.

If you are growing your tomatoes on the cordon system, there will come a time when you are sure to wonder how much taller you should let the plants grow. Generally speaking outdoor plants are stopped after they have made four or five trusses. After this the growing tip of the plant is removed. Count up from the top truss and remove the tip from above the second leaf. Actually you will have to decide for yourself at what point to stop the plants. Some varieties develop the fruits so quickly that you can take the plant up to six trusses. The Cura I grew this year of writing is one of these. The season also plays its part. The warmer it is and the longer the frosts stay at bay, the longer the plants will go on growing. Personally I am quite happy to be left with several trusses of green fruits by the time the plants must be scrapped. So long as the lower fruits are swelling I see no point in preventing the plant from producing more, even if at the end these are not as large as the lower ones. They are still useful, still edible.

If you have no suitable place where the plants can go in the ground, the best thing is either to make a special raised bed for them in some warm and sheltered spot, or to plant them in containers which can then be stood alongside a sunny wall, fence or hedge. A garage wall often offers a good site.

Ring culture is a good method of raising tomatoes either in the greenhouse or in some sheltered place outdoors. For this you should use bottomless pots. Whalehide pots are specially made for this purpose, cheap and expendable. These are then stood on a layer of well weathered ashes or clinker, or failing these, ordinary gravel or shingle is perfectly suitable. The pots should be filled with John Innes Potting Compost No. 2 or 3. Each container should hold one plant, which should be well staked and then grown as described above. The roots which grow at the base of the pot serve mainly to anchor the plants and those which grow into the whalehide serve to feed them and encourage the fruits.

Tomato plants in containers need generous supplies of water and food. In hot weather it may be necessary to water them three times a day and to damp them down, i.e., to spray or syringe them as frequently.

Turnips and swedes

When I think back to my youth, I remember how important turnips were to country people. Turnips figured large in gardens and allotments. I can remember the look of disbelief on my father's face when, newly come from London, his new country neighbour told him that when he awoke from his afternoon nap, 'I looks round for a turnip, and 'e do go down as sweet as a nut.'

The tops were valued as highly as the roots and I think that this might be one of the reasons for the decline in popularity because these greens are perhaps too strong for modern popular taste. However, they are rich in vitamins. It is not generally realised either that the leaves of swedes can be forced like chicory. They are good in salads or cooked like seakale.

Turnips are much like radish, they need to be grown quickly and in good soil if they are to be succulent. They will grow well in ordinary soil, but they do not like heavy soil. It must be well drained with plenty of humus. Turnips are brassicas.

The white turnip does not seem to be as hardy as the yellow-fleshed variety, probably because the latter have a little of the hardy swede in them. Varieties such as Golden Ball store best.

There are some varieties which will mature faster than others, such as White Milan, which is one of the earliest and the F1 hybrid Tokyo Cross. They should take some 8–10 weeks.

Early sowings do well under cloches. If you want young roots sow first in February and then at three week intervals until early July if you wish a continuous supply, although I should warn you that they are not always a successful summer crop. Like radishes they are affected by heat and drought.

Swedes should be sown in May and given similar treatment to turnips. Purple-top is a quick growing variety which stores well. It is also good to pull young. Swedes tend to take more space and if you have a small garden you may prefer the yellow fleshed turnips. There is not a great deal of difference between them when they are grated in salads or cooked and mashed.

If you like turnip tops you can raise a good crop for cutting by sowing Green-top White. These will give you bicoloured half green, half white roots and plenty of leaves to pick.

Sow in shallow drills and thin out early. Space rows 12ins apart.

6

CALENDAR OF GARDEN WORK AND CROPS AVAILABLE

JANUARY

Crops available
Fresh salads and greens. Broccoli in variety, brussels sprouts, cabbage including salad variety, winter cauliflower, celery, corn salad, dandelion, endive, kale, land cress, leaf beet, lettuce, savoy, winter spinach.
Fresh roots. Celeriac, kohl-rabi, leeks, parsnips, radish, salsify, scorzonera, swede, turnip.
Store roots. Beet, carrot, garlic, Hamburg parsley, onion, parsnip, shallot, salsify, scorzonera, swede.
Other items in store. Jerusalem artichoke, beans (haricot, butter, brown, etc.) marrow, pumpkin, squash.
Forced. Chicory, dandelion, rhubarb, seakale and all sprouting crops such as mustard and cress, alfalfa, fenugreek, mung beans, oats.

Garden work
This is not usually the best month for actual gardening, but there are several jobs you can do in preparation for the season ahead. Some can be done indoors. If you have a greenhouse, warmed frames, cloches, or for some things even wide window sills or some other warm and sunny place you can sow seeds of such crops as aubergine, brussels sprouts, french beans, summer cabbage to give a late spring crop, shorthorn carrots, leeks, lettuce, onions, radishes, tomatoes, and of course any of the sprouting crops. These are best grown in succession – see detailed notes. In a hot bed in a frame make the second sowing of long-rooted radish. Sow broad beans in a warm frame. Potatoes can be placed in trays in a garage, frost-free shed, box room or some similar light place.

It is a good plan now to inspect and oil garden tools and to send any that need it for servicing or maintenance. Check on supplies of labels, string, slug pellets. Get a good garden line. Send for seed catalogues and begin buying seeds.

In the garden an early broad bean, Aquadulce Claudia can be sown. Shallots can be planted from now until April.

Make certain that your soil is in good condition. If you are doubtful, buy and use a soil testing outfit. Test the soil in different parts of the garden and do this annually as it can change. If the soil needs lime now is the time to apply it. Use hydrated lime. Otherwise fork in slow acting manures, but never use both together. Spread well rotted composts and animal manure between the rows of plants so that this can help keep them warm now, and can be forked in later when the crops are cleared. Place a good deep mulch over the asparagus beds or over the plants.

Protect well formed broccoli or spring cauliflowers by snapping the midrib of an outer leaf or two to cover the curd like a roof.

Vegetables which can be forced outdoors include dandelion, rhubarb and seakale. Indoors you can force dandelion, chicory and seakale roots.

FEBRUARY

Crops available
Fresh salads and greens. As January.
Fresh roots. As January.
Store roots. As January.
Other items in store. As January.
Forced. As January.

Garden work
Indoors in warmth or under glass continue or begin to sow aubergines, french and broad beans, brussels sprouts, shorthorn carrots, cucumbers, celery and celeriac, cauliflowers, leeks, lettuce, onion, radish, tomatoes and all the sprouting crops. On a hot bed make another sowing of long-rooted radish.

Outdoors and at the end of the month many seeds may be safely sown so long as the soil is in good condition and so long as the garden is fairly sheltered. Otherwise it is best to use cloches or to wait. Those which can be sown include Early and Mangetout or Sugar peas, lettuces, radishes, onions, parsley, parsnips, round (i.e., summer) spinach and seakale. Broad beans and parsnips can go into the open ground. Garlic, onion sets and shallots can be planted. If your spring cabbages have failed, sow a quick maturing variety such as Carters Velocity in the rows where they are to mature. Do not transplant, thin out the seedlings instead to prevent giving the plants a check. Plant Jerusalem artichokes. You can use some of those you have in store. Lift and divide chives. Transplant autumn sown onions. In a warm, sheltered place you can plant a few early potatoes.

Continue to dig whenever possible and enrich the soil.

If they have been left in the soil parsnips will soon begin to grow again, so lift any you find and store or deep freeze them. This also applies to any other root crop you may be growing.

MARCH

Crops available
Fresh salads and greens. As January.
Fresh roots. Spring onions and as January.
Store roots. As January.
Other items in store. Swedes and as January.
Forced. As January.

Garden work
In warmth and under glass you can still sow aubergines, broad beans, brussels sprouts, broccoli, celery, celeriac, cauliflowers, cucumbers, courgettes, marrows, peppers, herbs of many kinds, radish, tomatoes for summer and autumn crops under glass or for planting outdoors and sweet corn.

On a hot bed in a frame make a final successional sowing of long-rooted radish.

Tomatoes and cucumbers to be grown in greenhouses should be planted now.

Dwarf beans sown in the ground under cloches in a sheltered garden will produce a very early crop and are less work than the pot-grown type later to be planted.

If you have no glass you will be wise to prepare a small raised nursery bed on which to sow brussels sprouts, leeks, cauliflowers and summer cabbages.

In the open and only if soil and weather conditions permit, sow broccoli in variety, broad beans, early carrots, cabbages, kohl-rabi, lettuce, land cress, onions, peas, parsley, parsnips, radishes, salsify and scorzonera, seakale, summer spinach, leaf beet, swiss chard, turnips. Sow beetroot at the end of the month unless you have some warm, cloche-covered soil available.

Plant Jerusalem artichokes, asparagus, brussels sprouts seedlings, spring cabbages, red cabbages, cauliflowers, chives, garlic, onion sets and autumn sown onions, potatoes, horse radish, rhubarb, shallots and seakale.

To spur them into growth give spring cabbages a tonic such as sulphate of ammonia, nitrate of soda or nitrochalk, about 1oz to a yard of row.

Spring clean the garden. Clear all decayed leaves from the ground, for they are likely to be harbouring insects. Put them with any weeds on the compost heap. Tidy and prepare each row as it becomes vacant to make it ready for the crop to come. Test to see if the soil needs lime when you do this.

APRIL

Crops available
Fresh salads and greens. Broccoli in variety, cabbages including salad type which should go on until early May, winter cauliflowers, celery, corn salad, land cress, leaf beet, kale, lettuce.
Fresh roots. Early carrots, celery, celeriac, leeks, radishes, spring onions.
Store roots. Probably the last of most of these, beetroot, carrots, onions, parsnips, swedes. Garlic and shallots should keep until this year's crop is ready, but inspect them from time to time. If you do not need them in the kitchen plant any which are sprouting.
Forced. Various sprouting crops.

Garden work
In warmth continue to sow or make a beginning with aubergines, dwarf and climbing beans of all kinds, celery, celeriac, courgettes, cucumbers, marrows, peppers, pumpkins, tomatoes, squash, sweet corn.

In the open sow asparagus, globe artichokes, beetroot, broad and dwarf beans, broccoli in variety, brussels sprouts, cabbages, carrots, cauliflowers, endive, Florence fennel, kale, kohl-rabi, leaf beet and swiss chard, lettuces, pickling onions, parsley and Hamburg parsley, peas including the asparagus or winged peas and Petit Pois, radishes, salsify and/ or scorzonera, savoy, seakale and turnips.

Plant asparagus roots, globe artichokes, broad bean plants raised under glass, cauliflowers, leeks, lettuces, onions including sets, peas raised in pots, second early and maincrop potatoes.

Prepare the stations and beds for any of the marrow family, courgettes, squash, outdoor cucumbers, etc.. Use this ground while you are waiting for the right season for catch crops of lettuce, radishes or even young carrots. Remember that you will be able to leave them there until the larger plants grow sufficiently to crowd them.

Check that you have supports for peas and beans.

Thin out seedlings where necessary. Prick out and transplant celery and begin hardening off this and other crops. Earth up potatoes. Stake peas. Lift the last of the celery and leeks.

MAY

Crops available
Fresh salads and greens. Asparagus, broccoli in variety, cabbage, winter cauliflower, leaf beet, kale, lettuces, peas (round), spinach.
Fresh roots. Carrots, celeriac, radishes, spring onions, turnips.

Garden work
A busy month this. At the end of the month you can plant out most of the

vegetables you have raised in warmth and you can gradually uncover crops grown under cloches unless there is still danger of frosts.

Outdoors you can sow all kinds of beans, beetroot, cauliflower, chicory, corn salad, cucumbers, kale, kohl-rabi, lettuces, any of the marrow family, pickling onions, peas of all kinds, radishes, spinach, leaf beet and swiss chard, seakale, swedes, sweet corn and turnips.

You can still plant potatoes. Thin other seedlings wherever necessary and transplant those in nursery beds which are large enough to handle.

Begin supporting peas and tall varieties of broad beans as soon as these are above ground. Earth up any very early potatoes, just covering the shoots with soil so as to protect them from any late frosts. They will soon grow through this soil.

Green, leafy plants such as lettuces and spinach and any of the brassicas may need a tonic at this time. Treat them as recommended in March.

JUNE

Crops available

Fresh salads and greens. Asparagus, broad and dwarf beans, summer broccoli, cabbage, summer cauliflower, courgettes, cucumber, leaf beet, lettuces, peas, spinach.

Fresh roots. Carrots, celeriac, kohl-rabi, onions, radishes, turnips.

Garden work

A good month for catching up and even for beginning. Sow dwarf and climbing beans where they are to mature, beetroots, shorthorn carrots, chinese cabbage, endive, Florence fennel, kohl-rabi, lettuces, early varieties of peas to mature in early autumn, sugar peas, pickling onions, radishes, summer spinach, sweet corn, swedes, turnips and outdoor cucumbers.

Meanwhile, if you have sown the last or any of the same family in pots indoors, now is the time to plant them out together with aubergines, beans, celery, celeriac, peppers, sweet corn and tomatoes.

Transplant any brassicas which are ready, even if they are very small. Little brussels sprout plants should go out into their final stations. Use the spaces between the plants for a catch crop of radishes.

If you can dibble the soil easily, begin planting leeks, dealing with the largest plants first. This will give you a natural succession.

Among the many miscellaneous jobs, earth up potatoes, give a tonic to root vegetables (best done after a rain shower or watering), feed cucumbers, and any of the marrow family and tomatoes.

Keep an eye on weeds and cut them down as soon as they show above ground.

JULY

Crops available
Fresh salads and greens. Artichokes (globe), cabbages, summer broccoli, cauliflowers, courgettes, cucumbers, kohl-rabi, land cress, leaf beet, lettuces, peas, broad, dwarf and climbing beans from cloche-protected plants, spinach, squash, early varieties of sweet corn.
Fresh roots. Beetroot, carrots, onions, potatoes, radishes, shallots, turnips.
Store roots. Autumn sown onions, shallots.

Garden work
You may be faced with a wet period or with drought. If it rains weeds grow apace, so take every chance that is offered to pull them up or cut them down. If there is a drought save all the water you can and give it to those plants which must grow fast such as radish and lettuce. If you notice that runner beans are not setting, syringe and water the plants each evening.

This month you can sow any seed except celery and celeriac, but the trouble with sowing any of the cucumber or marrow family is that the fruits may not mature before the cold autumn nights. However, if at that time you can protect them with cloches, go ahead with these also.

It might sound an odd time to sow parsnips, but if you have a little seed left over from the early spring sowing, sprinkle this thinly and pull the parsnips as young roots – they are delicious. Chinese cabbage and winter radishes may be sown now.

Plant kale and go on planting whatever is ready as advised last month. Support peas and beans.

If the weather is wet spray potatoes against blight. Autumn sown onions, shallots and possibly garlic may be lifted. Earth up celery, fennel, leeks and late potatoes.

AUGUST

Crops available
Fresh salads and greens. Artichokes (globe), aubergines, beans (broad, dwarf and climbing), summer broccoli, summer cabbage, cauliflowers, celery (Golden self-blanching), courgettes, cucumbers, Florence fennel, kohl-rabi, land cress, leaf beet and swiss chard, peas, peppers, spinach, squash, sweet corn (end of month), tomatoes.
Fresh roots. Beetroots, carrots, garlic, onions, radishes, turnips.
Store roots. As July.

Garden work
There are still a good many seeds which can be sown to ensure a supply of winter salads and green vegetables. Spring cabbage, red cabbage, corn

salad, endive, Florence fennel, land cress, lettuces, onions, radishes, sweet fennel, winter or prickly spinach, spinach beet and swiss chard, any of the sprouting crops and turnips.

Try to get most of the winter greens planted in their permanent places. Water them in well at the start if the weather is dry.

Early crops of endive should be ready to blanch. Earth up celery and leeks. Early beetroot can be lifted and stored. Onions should now be assisted to finish ripening. Bend their tops over to the shady side so the maximum sun reaches them. Gather any peas or beans for drying as they become ripe. Plants may be pulled and hung to dry.

SEPTEMBER

Crops available
Fresh salads and greens. Aubergines, beans (dwarf and climbing), broccoli, cabbages including red cabbage, autumn cauliflowers, self-blanching celery, courgettes, cucumbers, endive, Florence fennel, land cress, leaf beet and swiss chard, lettuces, marrows, peas, peppers, savoys, spinach, squash, sweet corn, tomatoes.
Fresh roots. Beetroot, carrots, Hamburg parsley, radishes, turnips, potatoes.
Store roots. Beetroot, carrots, onions, shallots, garlic.

Garden work
If you have a frame sow suitable cauliflower seed. Brussels sprouts sown now will give you very early crops next year, but take into consideration the value of the space involved. Under cloches or in warmth you can sow corn salad, endive, lettuce and radishes. In warmth sow any sprouting crops. Continue planting late winter and spring cabbages and continue blanching those crops which need it.

Look now to the store and begin lifting beetroots, carrots, marrows, onions, potatoes, pumpkins and squash. Note any which are not really ripe and leave them on the plants until frosts are imminent. Cut and separate them from the ripe ones so that these are used first, for they will not keep for long. They can be deep frozen of course.

Gather any green tomatoes left on the plants. Do not place them in the window to ripen, for they do this quicker in the dark. Put them in a drawer or a box with a lid. Inspect them from time to time and remove the red ones.

If the cauliflowers are forming heads or curds protect these from the sun and frost by snapping the midrib of an outside leaf which will then fall over the curd. Look out for late caterpillars. Pick them off and destroy them or they will eat the greens and the curds.

OCTOBER

Crops available

Fresh salads and greens. Beans, dwarf and climbing, possibly late crop of broad; broccoli, brussels sprouts, cabbage including the white winter salad types, autumn cauliflowers, celery self-blanching, corn salad, cucumbers, dandelions, endive, Florence fennel, land cress, leaf beet, lettuces, peas, savoys.
Fresh roots. Artichokes (Jerusalem), beetroot, carrot, celeriac, leeks, parsnips, Hamburg parsley, radishes, salsify and scorzonera, swedes, turnips.
Store roots. Beetroot, carrots, Hamburg parsley, parsnips, potatoes, swedes, turnips.
Other items in store. Dried beans, marrows, pumpkins, squash, tomatoes.
Forced. Chicory.

Garden work

You can still sow corn salad.

So much depends on the locality of your garden whether or not you lift and store your vegetables or leave them in the ground and dig them when required. It might be prudent to do both, and then should we experience really severe weather with frost bound soil, you will have some stores at hand. This being so, lift beet, carrots, swedes and turnips now.

Blanch and protect crops as advised last month. Plant cabbages. Pull off yellow leaves from all brassicas and make this routine from now on. Thin lettuce and transplant the seedlings in a warm spot or under cloches, 4ins apart.

Inspect the beans you hung up last month. As soon as they are dry enough you should start to shell them. Some may be ready before the others.

Cut back asparagus and globe artichoke stems.

There are a few peas which can be sown as early as this month to stand the winter and to produce a late spring crop. They include Unwins Histon Mini, Meteor and Superb, all round-seeded varieties. The first, dwarf, is an excellent variety for cloches, but beware of mice. Sow broad beans.

Lift some chicory roots and expose them to the air for a few days.

NOVEMBER

Crops available

Fresh salads and greens. Broccoli, brussels sprouts, cauliflowers, cabbage in variety, celery, corn salad, dandelion, endive, Florence fennel, kale, land cress, leaf beet, lettuce, savoy, winter spinach.
Fresh roots. Artichokes, celeriac, leeks, parsnips, Hamburg parsley, radishes, salsify, scorzonera, swedes, turnips.

Store roots. Artichokes, beetroot, carrots, garlic, onions, Hamburg parsley, parsnips, potatoes, shallots, salsify, scorzonera, turnips.
Other items in store. As last month.
Forced. Chicory, dandelion, rhubarb, seakale, and all sprouting crops (see January).

Garden work

If you live in the south, or in some sheltered, favoured spot, sow broad beans and round early peas. Earth up a little soil around the stems of spring cabbage and brussels sprouts. This gives them protection from strong winds. Alternatively, stake them with short canes thrust into the ground near the stem of the plant and against the wind.

Place protective material over the rows of root crops which are to be left in the soil. Check that no mice are eating them, and if so set traps. Cast a few slug pellets under the cloches against these other predators.

Dig and manure or lime, or mulch with dung or compost, all vacant ground as early in the month as possible so that it can be well weathered.

Lift Jerusalem artichokes, horseradish, parsnips and salsify so that you have some roots ready if the bad weather sets in. Lift the forcing roots of chicory, dandelion, rhubarb and seakale.

DECEMBER

Crops available

Fresh salads and greens. Broccoli, brussels sprouts, cabbages in variety, winter cauliflower, celery, corn salad, dandelion, endive, kale, land cress, leaf beet, lettuce, savoy, winter spinach.
Fresh roots. Carrots, celeriac, leeks, parsnips, radish, salsify, scorzonera, swede, turnip.
Store roots. Beet, carrot, garlic, Hamburg parsley, horse radish, onion, parsnip, potato, salsify, scorzonera, shallot, swede, turnip.
Other items in store. Artichokes, beans, marrow, pumpkin, squash.
Forced. As last month.

Garden work

Not really the best gardening month of the year. However, there are a few jobs which one ought not to leave undone. Blanch endives, draw up soil around late planted leeks. Protect the large curds of cauliflower and broccoli. Force salads and rhubarb. Inspect the store vegetables as one rotten specimen can contaminate many.

Look also at any seed packets you may be saving. Mice often find these.

Make a hot bed in a frame and sow the first of long-rooted radish. Sow broad beans in a warmed frame.

7

PERSONAL TOUCHES

It is only to be expected that after gardening for many years one discovers ways and means of easing some tasks, of taking short cuts, of cutting down on labour and of generally helping plants to grow a little faster, a little better. No doubt everyone has his or her pet methods. You have only to listen to two or three tomato growers gathered together to realise that this is so. Often what one thinks is a discovery proves later to be accepted practice somewhere else.

I would suggest that while it is wise to pay some respect to traditional methods, one should sometimes question them also, especially where in order to achieve the required ends the means involve considerable hard work. Rather than reject a vegetable because its cultivation seems beyond you, try to grow it some other way. You may not produce a prize winner, but the results may bring you satisfaction and you can always try to improve on your own methods. Remember also that because of the shortage of labour, other people's labour, housework has changed with the times and it is more than likely that there is much in gardening which could also be changed.

In our own garden we have a large area of grass which naturally needs mowing frequently, and this means a lot of work for my husband and me. Yet on the other hand the mowings help to save us work, for they are put to wide use. For instance, they are laid deep over the soil around shrubs so that they can help keep these plants moist at the roots and to smother weed seedlings, and so save us the job of continually cleaning around the roots. These mowings are also used in the vegetable garden, not only for mulches but to provide soil warmth as they decay.

I should point out that I am rather careful about which mowings I take into the vegetable garden. Obviously grass which has been treated with a weedkiller should never be used for a mulch but should be stacked somewhere so that it can lose its toxic qualities and become weathered and neutral before it is composted. Neither do I put the first two or three cuts of the year along the vegetable rows, simply because these are more likely to contain all the dross of winter, including weed seeds blown into the grass by wind or dropped by birds.

These cuttings are then placed down between the rows of vegetables, not so close that they come up to the stems of the plants, but so that they cover most of the space between the rows. It is best to begin by placing the grass at the nearest end of the row so that as you proceed along it you walk on the laid grass and not on the soil. The grass forms a good mat and prevents the soil from becoming panned. Should you wish later to sow some seed in the covered space, it is quite simple to pull the mulch aside. Under it the soil will be moist and receptive so that a drill is soon made.

In spring when I want to sow or perhaps plant those tender half hardy vegetables such as all the marrow family and beans, I make a drill or a hole as the case may be, deeper and wider than it otherwise need be. Should the season be dry, or if the site has been cloche-covered, the drill or hole is first watered. This depression is then lined with fresh lawn mowings, trodden down so that they are well packed. On this grass layer is spread a cover of peat and/or good soil, to bring the drill or hole up to the required depth for seed sowing or planting. The seed is sown and is then covered with a little more peat or good soil.

The grass ferments and soon warms up the soil and creates a type of gentle hot bed. The source of heat is down far enough for it to be well away from the newly emerging roots. By the time they have grown enough to reach the lower levels, the first heat will have subsided. Because of the nature of the lawn mowings the heat is a moist one.

This question of creating, capturing and maintaining heat in the early stages of certain seeds and plants is important. By sowing seed where the plants are to mature you can with protection save work and raise earlier crops. Squash is a vegetable that does best sown where it is to grow.

If you have no cloches you can use large glass jars and any clear, strong plastic vessel or container as a covering for one seed, for a small group of seeds or for a young plant. The jars should be left in place until the plants are actually crowding them. The leaves should never rest against the glass or they will be liable to scorch. Usually by this time the frosts are over. Provide ventilation and gradually harden the plant by raising the rim of the jar from the soil, just slipping a stone or a piece of wood under it. Let in a little more air each day. In some seasons you can uncover the plants by day and put the glass on them at night.

I am always thinking of what short cuts I can take when sowing seed, a sentiment which I fear would make many an old time gardener turn in his grave since seed sowing is often so ritualistic. But then, he had only to garden, whereas I, like so many people today, have to fit the garden in with many other daily tasks, so the more time saved, the better. For instance, because we like radishes I sow ounces of this seed during the year, but I seldom sow a row on its own. Instead, almost every time I sow a new row of some vegetable, some radish seeds go in with it. The radish is sown in the same drill, often but not always at the same depth. Since I have found that it grows so much better when there is peat in the soil, I find that it is usually best to sow the main vegetable, then to cover this lightly with peat and finally go along the row sprinkling the radish seed. I like to water this in after it has been covered. The radish seed always shows above ground first, which is often a great help if you want to get ahead with mulching or weeding. It is good to see the early sown crops well defined. When radish is sown with parsnip which takes a long time to mature, the row is soon defined and you can go ahead and plan crops to grow nearby. By the time the host crop is growing well, or needs more space, the radish should have been harvested and out of the way.

I do not mix radish with onions or peas, and when I sow carrots I find it best simply to broadcast some radish along between their rows rather than to sow in the same drill. This is to prevent attacks of onion or carrot root fly. If I grew radish with peas, the young seedlings would cling to the radish.

Drawing seed drills takes considerable time, sometimes effort too. If the soil is in good condition you should be able to dibble in some of the larger seeds instead of drawing drills for them, such as beans of all kinds and large pelleted seed. Potatoes can be dibbled or planted in with a trowel at the correct intervals.

Most vegetables are sown where they are to mature. The exceptions are those kinds that take a long time to develop, and as a rule we keep these in some place where they can wait until another crop is finished. For these we make a nursery bed. Yet many of us find that it is less work in the long run, if instead of transplanting the seedlings back into the nursery bed, we plant them in their rows even though they may be quite small. There is no need to waste the seemingly large space between each of these tiny plants. These spaces can be used to produce catch crops of some plant which will not smother nor rob the seedling, plants such as lettuce, radish or corn salad. Alternatively you can transplant the seedlings into a thick row at one of the permanent sites and space them out later, leaving an established row, correctly spaced, which will mature earlier than those rows made from the transplanted plants. Or these spaces could be used as temporary nursery areas where seeds can be grown to be transplanted as soon as these too can be handled. These include such things as endive, lettuce and cauliflower.

On the other hand there are times when brassicas are jostling each other in their nursery rows and there is no room for them to go across the plot in their rows. I plant them anywhere for the time being, down the side of the plot for example, at the edge like an edging. They are not really in the way, for you can always step over them to get on to the plot and between the other rows.

It seems to me that the larger the vegetable, often the greater the waste in top foliage or outside leaves there is in proportion. True the trimmings can go on to the compost heap, but surely more vegetables, though smaller in size, would be more acceptable? Extra large vegetables are seldom of high quality, nor do they taste so well as the younger, smaller kinds, and they are also difficult to prepare for cooking.

In my own garden crops are grown so closely that I often have to tread carefully for fear of damaging some. I am never more pleased than when rows of plants touch fingertips, as it were. I believe that if ground covers are beneficial in a flower garden then there surely is a role for them to play in a vegetable patch. The crops I raise from these plants suit me and my way of cooking, although they are not likely to carry off first prizes at a vegetable show.

Whether or not you space the vegetables to the measurements given on the seed packets, or whether you decide like me to grow them closer in most cases, do remember that the more food you produce to the square yard the more you should feed and care for your soil.

Many of the modern vegetables are so compact that the old spacing measurements are out of date. Take neat varieties of brussels sprouts and winter cabbage for example, I simply plant these two trowel lengths apart in their rows. Most of my rows are my foot length, 9ins, apart. Where root vegetables are concerned, I expect them to be touching in the rows. These are sown thinly, given a first early thinning to separate them so that each plant has its own living room, then as I need them alternate plants are pulled or those which have obviously grown faster, even if the roots are quite small. So long as they are usable they are worth having, and after all even a tiny vegetable shows a profit on just one seed. This thinning leaves a little more space for those that are left to expand. As these grow, or as more roots are required, the same process is followed until they are more widely spaced. This seems to me to be more economic than thinning the seedlings early to wide spaces between them and then throwing away the thinned-out plants.

I also keep rows fairly close, sometimes closer than my 9ins foot length. At one time this was considered to be somewhat foolhardy by some of my gardening friends, even though the results were there for them to see. Now, I am happy to say, my findings are borne out by garden research scientists, who among other things have shown that onions raised in rows 9ins apart with just 2ins between the plants, and carrots sown 4ins between the rows and 3ins between the plants, give a high yield of medium sized roots. Medium in the case of onions is about the size of a tennis ball, large enough for most cooks I imagine.

It seems to me that one factor in the yield per square yard is seldom considered. Most of the private gardener's practices have come down to us from the days when the gardener was only one of the staff maintained by a normal middle class household. This gardener was a paid servant and as such he did not have to buy seeds, implements, fertilisers or any of the materials he used. But the most important thing of all is that he did not have to buy, nor did he have any idea of the value of, the land he was working. As a rule he had plenty of space and from the land he produced more than enough for the family and the servants. Today that same land has probably increased tenfold in value, perhaps more and it is therefore more than ever necessary to grow from it the greatest possible quantity of food that is compatible with flavour and nourishment, and the amount of labour and time that can be expended on it. This is more than a personal duty, I feel, it is a national and international obligation. If we have land, however small a plot, we hold it in trust on behalf of our fellow men.

Techniques are a great help, and one important thing is to learn to sow thinly and appreciate the importance of thinning out seedlings so that they are separated from groups into individuals. If this is not done the crowded plants become tough or rush to flower. Disease sets in among them or pests infest them.

You need not waste all the thinnings if you are of an economical turn of mind. Those of leaf vegetables can be transplanted, although not many people bother to transplant spinach or leaf beet. I have to do this from time to time to make up the gaps in a row where a mole has lifted portions of it in its search for worms. On the continent swiss chard is transplanted when it is quite large. Lettuce should be thinned as early as possible to avoid botrytis, a disease which is liable to attack crowded plants, es-specially where slugs are present. If you thin these in stages you can use the young plants as salads while you are waiting for the larger plants to mature.

The best time to thin, always, is when the soil is moist but not sodden. If there is a drought, water the row a little while before thinning.

Transplanting with a dibber is quick and does for leeks and some of the tough brassicas when these do not have a good root ball, for plants you buy in bundles for instance. Generally, though, I think it worth while to spend time and trouble on transplanting. Even for brassicas I like to make a hole a little larger than necessary and to fill it with a little extra good soil or peat with a little balanced fertiliser mixed with it. If the roots are then well watered in and the new soil covered with the garden earth and the plant firmed in it suffers little check.

Plants which have been grown on in pots can be helped considerably by the following method. Take a flower pot the same size as the pot in which the plant is growing. Scoop out a depression in the soil larger than the pot and fill this with peat. Put the pot in so that its rim is at soil level and press it so that when you take it out from the peat it has left its own shape. Gently knock the plant from its pot and fit it into its new pot-shaped hole. Water it in and cover the peat with soil.

When you transplant lettuce, endive and chicory, keep an eye on the seed leaves, the first which were formed by the plant. These will be very small. When you transplant, never bury these but leave them always sitting on the soil.

And speaking of lettuce, two other points. In summer during drought, water the lettuce the evening before you cut it in the morning. If water is scarce, just look after three plants at a time so that these grow succulent. When you have cut one, move along the row to take in the next plant. Cut the largest first, of course.

In spring and autumn (it is not worth while in summer) you can keep lettuce going a little longer by cutting the head and leaving the root stump in the soil. This will sprout. You will not get several headed lettuces as a result, but you will get plenty of shoots which are welcome in winter salads.

The same applies to cabbages. To ensure some spring greens, and so long as you are willing to let the old plant occupy the space, cut out the heart only, leaving some outside leaves. With a knife cut a cross in the top of the cut surface of the stem. Make this cut about a ¼in deep. This will encourage the buds in the axils of the cabbage leaves to grow. It is not worth keeping cauliflowers once you have cut these.

Perpetual spinach sown in spring can be carried forward to the following spring, at which time it will then begin to go to seed. It is hardy enough to stand the winter uncovered, but I have found the following method gives a heavier crop and more succulent leaves. In autumn before the nights become really cold, cut the crop hard, leaving the centres, and cover them with a cloche. In two or three weeks there should be enough new leaves to cut again. Keep the plants covered until spring and you will be able to cut some on most winter days.

If you sow a row of corn salad, or plant lettuce or endive near the spinach, the same cloche can cover both crops. Alternatively, sow carrot near it in late July. If the carrots are kept covered they need not be lifted and stored.

A word about my way of growing shallots so that I always have some young ones at hand and so that I get the greatest value from the crop no matter how small were some of the bulbs when lifted.

Good sound shallots should keep all year until the new crop is lifted. When I clean them I set aside any very small bulbs, and as I use them I also set aside any of the tiny bulbs one sometimes finds clinging to a larger bulb under the same outer skin. I use these little bulbs to plant in succession throughout the season.

I begin by planting all that is left of the old crop when I lift the new. I simply dibble individual bulbs in wherever I have space, down the side of the path, in between lettuces, in any odd spot. They sprout quickly, and as soon as one batch is about 2ins high I dibble in some more.

These give me a continuous crop of green top 'scallions'. I can use them in salads as spring onions, or in cooking. The tops can be finely sliced and used like chives in winter, and they can be used to flavour soups and sauces. Each tiny bulb grows and multiplies, so even if its bulbs do not become very large, you still show a profit. However, most of these tiny bulbs produce several good sized bulbs, and of course these grow larger the longer you leave them. They are quite hardy.

Now the vexed question of pea sticks. It is possible instead of twiggy sticks to use bamboo canes and thread or string. Push the canes in vertically along each side of the row some inches apart. Pass the thread round each one at one end and along one side and then back the other, just a few inches above the soil level. This will give a hold for the first tendrils and will also help to keep the birds off. Next fasten the thread a little higher up and this time, after going along each side of the row, take the twine zigzag across the canes from side to side. This will give a hold to the tendrils at the centre. Continue this way until the supports are high enough, i.e. a little higher than the given height of the pea plants.

For some years now I have also been using some plastic covered wire edging, the type usually put along the edge of paths to keep people off the grass or the garden. This is in a roll and it is sometimes a nuisance to handle. The idea is that you simply push the wire legs into the soil at intervals, but a long roll is sometimes inclined to have a will of its own. However, it is possible to buy the same type of edging in shorter lengths. If you think the initial outlay worth while I would recommend it. It will last almost for ever and it supports the plants very well, besides which it takes so little time to install.

So far as chemical pesticides are concerned I have mixed feelings. Certainly I try not to use them, but there are times when I feel that I must. But before I take a spray or a powder off the shelf I make sure that there is not some other means I could use. Apart from anything else, one has to consider the cost. To do all we are sometimes advised to do would mean using a great many different kinds of sprays and powders and maintaining a small chemist's store in the garden shed. All of these cost money which must be subtracted from the value of your produce. It might be cheaper to buy your food!

On the other hand some soils seem full of every noisesome pest, as was my own soil in the early days of making the vegetable garden. Radish was always smothered with flea beetles the moment it appeared above soil, carrots were riddled with one tiny worm or another, cauliflowers and cabbage crawled with caterpillars and there were slugs everywhere. Until I began to dust the seedlings or the seed rows when sowing I never had a sound radish or carrot. On the other hand, the soil itself is now so much cleaner and healthier that there must be a better balance of soil life, and certainly pests are not so rife, but then our garden is not surrounded by others. As the vegetable plot is under cover I cannot rely on the birds to keep down some of the pests, but there are many ladybirds which deal with much of the aphis. For instance in this year of writing we never once found aphis on lettuce and one meets with agreeable little insects at all times on various plants or among grey aphis on brassicas. One also sees hunting centipedes, spiders and others.

Rather than use spray or powder pesticides frequently and also to keep down costs, we have arranged that the pipe which drains the water from the washing machine does not flow away into the general drainage system during the warmer months but that it is instead collected in two large plastic dustbins, soapy water in one and the rinse water in the other. We change the pipe over at half time. All the soapy water is used on brassicas and on broad beans. This serves largely to keep them free from caterpillars and aphis. The other water is used for lettuces, seedlings and other plants. I use watering cans with a fine rose to apply the water. It is a bit of a chore carrying the water to the garden but the results are worth while and the remedy is cheap. In this year of writing, except for slug pellets no other pesticide has been used in the vegetable garden.

Obviously this whole subject of pesticides is something about which everyone must make a personal decision. Pests can become troublesome, and if you have neighbours with dirty gardens yours too is likely to suffer. Most of us, whatever our feelings, cannot afford to stand by and see the fruits – and the roots and leaves – of our labours consumed and spoiled. As with most other things it becomes necessary to compromise. There is some basic information on pests and diseases in the next chapter.

8

PESTS AND DISEASES

The researching, preparation, testing, manufacture and marketing of pesticides, fungicides and herbicides is a multi-million pound industry aimed mainly at farmers and commercial growers but taking in also the considerable amateur gardener sector. It is one which has enabled food products to be produced on a scale which without its products would be quite impossible. In general terms it could be said that the industry tries to produce preparations directed towards the control of a single pest or disease, so that when applied no other possibly beneficial insect or virus would be harmed. On the other hand, the demand of the mainly amateur cultivator has been for a single preparation with so broad a spectrum that all harmful pests would be eliminated by a single application. This conflict of interests has led to a certain amount of damage being done, some of which was at one time so serious that the rightful outcry of conservationists led to the banning or control of certain preparations which had in the past been of the greatest possible benefit to mankind. It was not so much the preparations which were at fault as the careless or uncontrolled manner in which they were used.

The problem for the beginner vegetable gardener is to suggest which preparations will be most useful to him in preventing, curing or clearing diseases and pests in his plot, preparations which are as safe as possible, as quick in their action and as brief in their life, preparations which do not taint vegetable flavours and which are simple to apply.

These preparations depend on the pests and diseases likely to be encountered by the gardener. Fortunately there are comparatively few and most can be prevented or cleared by the application of either an insecticide or a fungicide. The best way to prevent damage by insects or harm from disease is to grow your plants so that they are strong and healthy and to keep the environment clean and cleared of rubbish which harbours pests and disease spores.

Vegetables are somewhat different from flowers, for the former are grown to be eaten. It is necessary then that in treating vegetables for pests or diseases care should be taken that the pesticide or fungicide used can cause neither harm nor repugnance when the product is eaten. On packets or bottle of all products it is normal to see directions as to how soon a crop may be eaten after it has been treated and this direction must be carefully followed. Certain pesticides, however, are systemic, which is to say that they are absorbed by the plant and taken into the sap stream, and although this is advantageous in that attack by leaf chewing or sap sucking insects is curbed over a long period, it also means that the crop cannot be consumed by humans for some time. This point is normally covered by the fact that systemic insecticides are applied some time before the crop will be harvested and they will be cleared from the plant system by the time it is consumed.

The Ministry of Agriculture maintains a careful watch on chemicals for the farmer and gardener, and although manufacturers themselves subject their products to the most stringent tests before permitting them to go on the general market, the Ministry goes even further and insists that all new products or formulations are tested and approved by their scientists before they can be sold to the public. Approved products bear prominently on their labels the letter A surmounted by a crown.

Responsibility for the correct use of pesticides and fungicides must nevertheless rest with the user. Remember that a number of these are necessarily poisons, so treat them with great respect. Follow this set of invariable rules: Buy small quantities rather than large, so you don't have strange, half-filled bottles or packets in the shed which have lost their labels. Keep garden chemicals in a safe place out of reach of children and animals. Read labels carefully and follow directions meticulously. Use the correct product for the correct purpose and do not use persistent chemicals where short term alternatives are equally effective. Do not allow drift of chemicals, sprays or dusts on to other areas of the garden. Never spray when there is danger of killing bees or other beneficial insects. Clean all equipment after use and where possible keep special sprayers for special purposes. Safely dispose of all empty containers and never transfer pesticides into other containers such as milk bottles or those used for soft drinks. Wash all exposed parts of the body after spraying or dusting with pesticides.

The following lists mention and identify the pests and diseases most likely to be encountered and suggest cures or controls. Well grown plants, strong and healthy, will tend to escape or shrug off most of the diseases and some of the pests.

Pest or disease	Description	Plants affected	Control
Aphids	Clusters of green, grey or black sucking insects on foliage and stems.	Many, but mainly cabbages, beans.	Spray with soapy water, derris, BHC or malathion or use systemics based on demeton-methyl, dimethoate, formothion or menazon.
Blight	Wet black patches or blotches on foliage, tubers or fruit.	Mainly potatoes and tomatoes.	Preventive sprays of copper (Bordeaux mixture) or zineb from beginning July.
Cabbage root fly	Small white grubs on roots.	Cabbages and other brassicas.	Dust or water soil around plants with BHC or dip roots in calomel paste when planting.
Canker	Black or rusty portions at top of roots.	Parsnips	Choose resistant varieties; grow crop in fresh soil; control carrot root fly.
Carrot fly	Yellow grubs in roots.	Carrots mainly, but sometimes in parsley and parsnips.	Dress seed with BHC and put this also along rows.
Caterpillars	Typical, producing holes in leaves.	Cabbages mainly, but other brassicas too.	Spray or dust with derris, carbaryl or trichlorphon; pick off by hand.
Celery fly	Maggots making white blisters.	Celery, parsley and parsnips.	Spray with malathion, trichlorphon.
Club root	Swollen, large and misshapen roots.	Turnips and brassicas generally.	Sow on fresh soil; dip roots in calomel paste when planting.
Cutworms	Grey caterpillars on roots just below soil.	Any plant.	Dig BHC or carbaryl into top of soil at 1oz per sq yd.
Flea beetle	Small holes in leaves and dead seedlings.	Cabbages, radishes, turnips, etc.	Dust or spray with BHC or carbaryl.
Leatherjackets	Brown or grey grubs just below soil level.	Any plant.	Dig BHC or carbaryl into top soil at 1oz per sq yd.
Mildew	Soft white dust or mould on leaves, stems and fruits.	Peas and others.	Spray with dinocap fungicide and keep plants watered.

Pest or disease	Description	Plants affected	Control
Millepedes	Slow, many-legged insects that chew seeds and roots.	Any plant.	Dig BHC into soil.
Onion Fly	White grubs tunnelling into bulb bases.	Onions and shallots.	Dip roots in calomel before planting; dust calomel along rows.
Pea moth	Pea and bean weevil.	Bite marks in leaf edges.	Dust plants with carbaryl.
Root aphids	Grey insects on roots.	Lettuce.	Water plants with BHC or malathion solution.
Whitefly	White insects flying up when disturbed.	Brassicas and others.	Spray with dimethoate or malathion.
White rot	Leaves yellowing, white growth at base of bulbs.	Onions, leeks, etc.	Grow resistant varieties; try fresh soil; treat drills and roots with calomel.
Wireworms	Yellow grubs on roots or tubers.	Any plant.	Dig BHC dust into topsoil, but do not grow potatoes or other root crops in treated soil.

Note: Because chemical names are confusing, sometimes difficult to pronounce and occasionally unknown by shopkeepers, the following are some of the best known proprietary names for the products mentioned in the table above:

BHC – Boots BHC; Lindex Garden Spray; Murphy Gamma-BHC Dust.
Calomel – PBI Calomel Dust.
Carbaryl – Chlordane 25; Murphy Ant Killer.
Copper – Bordeaux Mixture.
Demeton-methyl – Metasystox.
Derris – Murphy Liquid Derris; PBI Derris Dust.
Dimethoate – Murphy Systemic Insecticide; Pestox.
Dinocap – Karathane Mildew Fungicide; Mildan.
Formothion – Toprose Systemic Spray.
Malathion – Murphy Liquid Malathion; PBI Malathion.
Menazon – Abol-X.
Trichlorphon – Dipterex 80.
Zineb – Dithane; Shell Zineb.
Names change frequently in gardening chemicals, but these should give an indication of the preparation you seek.

INDEX

Bold page numbers indicate major references

Acid soil 10
Air warming 41
Alfalfa 35, 96
Alkaline soil 10
All the Year Round, cauliflower 64
Amateur, tomato 98
American Green, celery 66
Amstel, carrot 62
Annual weeds 25
Apple cucumber 32
Apple mint 37
Aquadulce, broad bean 46
Arctic King, lettuce 79
Armoured cable, for soil warming 40
Arran Banner, potato 91
Arran Pilot, potato 91
Artichoke, Jerusalem **43**
Asparagus 33, **43**
Asparagus peas **90**
Aubergines **45**
Automatic timers, for soil warming 41
Autumn preparation of soil 22
Autumn Spear, broccoli 57
Avonresister, parsnip 86

Baby Crookneck, marrow or squash 33, 81
Backyard 31
Barletta Barla, onion 85
Basic slag 15
Beans, broad 39, **46**
Beans, french, kidney **or haricot 48**
Bean shoots 35
Beans, Mung 35
Beans, runner 50
Bedding fork 20
Beet, leaf 54
Beetroot 38, **53**
Big Boy, tomato 98
Black polythene sheeting 22
Blue Coco, french bean 48
Boltardy, beetroot 53

Bone flour 15
Bone meal 15
Bonfire 14
Border fork 19
Boron 16
Brassicas 12
British All Rounder, brussels sprout 58
Broccoli **55**
Brussels sprouts 57
Burpees Golden Beet 53
Burpless Early Green, cucumber 71
Burpless Green King, cucumber 71
Burpless Tasty Green, cucumber 71
Bush marrows 31
Butterhead, lettuce 78

Cabbage **59**
Cabbage, Chinese **61**
Cabbage, Red **60**
Cabbage, savoy **61**
Calabrese, summer broccoli 57
Calcifuges 37
Calcium 16
Carbonate of potash 14
Carrots 38, **61**
Carters Granda, french bean 50
Catch crops 44
Cauliflowers 39, **64**
Celeriac **65**
Celery **66**
Chalk 8, 10, 11
Champion Scarlet Horn, carrot 62
Chard, ruby 55
Chard, Swiss 54
Cheltenham Green-top, beetroot 53
Chickweed 8, 25
Chicory **67**
China Rose, radish 93
Clay 8, 9
Cleavers 8
Climbing beans 32
Cloches 37

Cloches, Novolux plastic 37
Coal ashes 14
Cold frame 39
Compost 8
Compost, garden 12
Compost heap 13
Compost, home made 12
Comtesse de Chambord, french bean 50
Convolvulus 9, 24
Copper 16
Corn salad 68
Couch grass 9, 24
County Horticultural Adviser 10
Courgettes 31
Cress, American 69
Cress, curled 69
Cresses 69
Cress, land 69
Cress, mustard and 69
Crisp Heart, lettuce 78
Crops, winter 39
Cucumbers 32, 38, 39, 71
Cultivator 27
Custard marrow 32
Czar, The, runner bean 51

Dandelions 24, 73
Desirée, potato 91
Dibber 17, 28
Digging fork 17
Diquat 20
Disabled Living Foundation 18
Dobies catalogue 50
Dobies Housewives Choice, beetroot 53
Dock 24
Double digging 23
Draw hoe 26
Dried blood 15
Dust mulch 22
Dwarf french beans 38

Earliest, cabbage 59
Early carrots 34
Early Dwarf, brussels sprout 58
Early Half Tall, brussels sprout 58
Early Purple Sprouting, broccoli 56
Early White Sprouting, broccoli 57
Ecballium elaterum 71
Electricity 40
Endive 34, 74
Epicure, potato 91

Fasolt Novelty, brussels sprout 58
Fat hen 8
Feltham First, pea 88, 89
Fennel 37

Fenugreek 35, 96
Fertilisers 15
Fertilisers, balanced 16
Fertilisers, inorganic 15
Fertilisers, organic 15
Fertilisers, proprietary 15
Fir Apple Pink, potatoe 91
Flageolets, french bean 48
Flora Blanca Algromajo No. 2, cauli-
    flower 64
Florence fennel 75
Fork, bedding 20
Fork, border 19
Fork, digging 17
Fork, manure 19
Formaldehyde 15
Frame, cold 39
Frame, cold, lean-to 40
Frame, cold, lights 40
French Breakfast, radish 93
Fuseau, Jerusalem artichoke 43

Garden compost 12
Garlic 31
Giant Seville, broad bean 46
Golden Acre, cabbage 59
Golden Ball, turnip 101
Golden Courgette 81
Golden Delicious, squash 81
Golden Queen, tomato 98
Goosefoot 8
Grand Rapids, lettuce 78
Grassland 24
Grass mowings 11
Green Bush, marrow 80
Green manure 25
Green-top White, turnip 101
'Gro-Bags' 32
Groundsel 8, 25

Hammonds Dwarf Scarlet, runner bean
    51
Heating wires, for soil warming 40
Heathers 37
Herb bank 36
Histon Cropper, tomato 98
Hoe 17, 26
Hoe, draw 26
Hoe, swan neck 27
Hogweed 24
Hoof and horn 15
Home Guard, potato 91
Humus 8, 10

Imperial Winter, lettuce 79
Innes, John, soil mixture 41

Iron 16
Italian Sprouting, broccoli 57

January King, cabbage 60
Jaune d'Hollande, potato 91
John Innes soil mixture 41

K symbol for potassium 16
Kale 76
Kerimure, soil-less compost 41
King Edward, potato 91
Kohl-rabi 76

Lady's fork 19
Land cress 25
Lawn 24
Lawn mowings 10
Late Purple Sprouting, broccoli 57
Late White Sprouting, broccoli 57
Leaf beet 31, 54
Leafmould 12
Leeks 77
Lettuce 78
Lettuce, winter 34, 38
Levington soil-less compost 41
Lime 10, 16, 27
Lime haters 37
Little Gem, marrow 81
Little Marvel, pea 89
Loam 8
Lobjoits Green Cos, lettuce 79
Long Black Spanish, radish 93
Long Green Trailing, marrow 80
Long White Trailing, marrow 81

Magnesium 16
Maize 97
Majestic, potato 91
Mangetout, pea 89
Manganese 16
Manure 8, 9
Manure, cow 10
Manure fork 19
Manure, green 25
Manure, horse 10
Manure, pig 10
Manure, stable 10
Marmande, tomato 98
Marrow 38, 80
Marus Piper, potato 91
May Express, cabbage 59
Melissa 37
Meteor, pea 89
Mi-chihili, Chinese cabbage 61
Midget, The, dwarf broad bean 46
Millet 35

Molybdenum 16
Moss 11
Mulch 8, 11, 12, 20
Mung beans 35, 96
Muriate of potash 15
Mustard and cress 96

N, symbol for nitrogen 16
National Vegetable Research Station 86
Nettles 24
Nitrate of soda 15
Nitro-chalk 15
Nitrogen 15

Oats 35, 96
Onions 83
Outdoor Girl, tomato 98
Outdoor tomatoes 38, 99

P, symbol for phosphorus 16
Paraquat 20
Paris Silver Skin, onion 85
Parsnips 85
Patio 31
Pattypan, squash 81
Peas 38, 87
Peas, asparagus 90
Peas, round 38
Peat 8, 10, 12
Peat hill 37
Peer Gynt, brussels sprout 58
Pentland Crown, potato 91
Perennial weeds 24
Perpetual spinach 31
Petit Pois, pea 89
Pe-Tsai, Chinese cabbage 61
pH 10
Phosphates 15
Potash 15
Potassium 15
Potatoes 12, 90
Potatoes, early 38
Potatoes, to clean ground 21
Proprietary fertilisers 15
Purple Sprouting, broccoli 57
Purple Podded, pea 89

Radish 38, 93
Rake 17, 27
Red cabbage 60
Remontante strawberries 33
Rhododendrons 37
Roodnerf Early Button, brussels sprout 58
Roodnerf-Vremo Inter, brussels sprout 58

Rotation of crops 25
Rotovator 24
Round Black Spanish, radish 93
Royal Horticultural Society 10
Ruby chard 55
Runner beans, 33, 38
Rye 35, 96

Salad Bowl, lettuce 78
Salsify **94**
Sand 8
Saynor hoe 26
Scorzonera **94**
Seakale beet 54
Seaweed 10
Seed raising 41
Sesame 35
Shallots 30, **95**
Sharpes Express, potato 91
Shelter 36
Shepherds purse 25
Silver beet 54
Slugs 9
Soil 7, 8
Soil, acid 10
Soil, alkaline 10
Soil clay 9
Soil, heavy 8
Soil, light 8
Soil, medium 8
Soil mixture, John Innes 41
Soil, neutral 8
Soil, ordinary 7
Soil, sour 8
Soil structure 20
Soil testing kit 10
Soil warming 40
Sowthistles 8
Soybeans 35, 96
Spade 17
Spinach **95**
Spit 18
Sprouting crops **96**
Sprouting shallot 33
Squash 31
Squash, golden 33
Straw 9
Strawberries, Remontante 33
Sugar peas 89
Sulphate of ammonia 14, 15
Sulphate of magnesium 15
Sulphate of potash 15, 16
Sulphur 16
Sunflower 96
Superphosphate of lime 15
Suttons Express Corona, broccoli 57

Suttons Sweetness, pea 89
Suttons Unrivalled, lettuce 78
Suttons Windermere, lettuce 79
Swan neck hoe 27
Swedes **101**
Sweet corn 33, 38, 97
Swiss chard 54

Thermostat, for soil warming 41
Thompson and Morgan 96
Tiny Tim, tomato 98
Tokyo Cross, turnip 101
Tomatoes **97**
Tomatoes, outdoor 38
Tools 17
Trace elements 14
Trowel 17, 28
Turk's cap gourd 32
Turnips **101**
Turves, rotted 8

Ulster Chieftan, potato 91
Unwins Dwergina, beetroot 53
Unwins Formanova, beetroot 53
Unwins Mini, pea 89
Urea-form 15

Valdor, lettuce 79
Vegetable refuse 10
Vegetable spaghetti, gourd 81
Veitch's Autumn Giant, cauliflower 64

Wall, for shelter 36
Wart disease, of potatoes 91
Webbs Wonderful, lettuce 78
Weedkiller 21
Weedol 9, 21
Weeds 11, 26
Wheat 35, 96
White Bush, marrow 81
White Icicle, radish 93
White Milan, turnip 101
White Stringless, runner bean 51
Winter crops 39
Winter Density, lettuce 79
Winter lettuce 34
Winter Salad, cabbage 60
Wire netting cage 36
Wonder Cross, Chinese cabbage 61
Wongbok, Chinese cabbage 61

Yellow Bush Scallop, squash 81
Yellow Perfection, tomato 98

Zinc 16